Praise for Dawn Starks

and

Simplify Your

FINANCIAL LIFE

"In *Simplify Your Financial Life*, Dawn Starks aligns the idea of leading a simpler, more minimalist life with the goal of tackling your financial life in easy-to-digest tips that anyone can understand and put into place. She makes simplifying your financial life surprisingly entertaining."

—JOSHUA BECKER, Founder of Becoming Minimalist
and author of *The Minimalist Home*

"*Simplify Your Financial Life* is a powerful book full of valuable lessons and tactical next steps that you can quickly integrate into your own life to live more with less. Dawn's lived it, and it shows in her clear, concise, high-value tips—even implementing just a few can have a radical impact on your life."

—GRANT SABATIER, Creator of Millennial Money
and author of *Financial Freedom*

"Dawn has taken her years of expert experience and packaged her wisdom into bite-size tips that will improve your financial life. Her down-to-earth tone and practical strategies show you how to take control of your budget, build wealth, and streamline your finances."

—FARNOOSH TORABI, Financial expert
and host of the *So Money* podcast

104 Easy Tips for Creating
the Abundant Future You Desire

Simplify Your FINANCIAL LIFE

DAWN G. STARKS

RIVER GROVE
BOOKS

The information contained in this book is meant to be educational in nature and is not meant to provide tax, legal, or investment advice to individuals. Laws change frequently and everyone's situation is unique. The information has been obtained from sources considered to be reliable, but we do not guarantee that the foregoing material is accurate or complete. Any information is not a complete summary or statement of all available data necessary for making an investment decision and does not constitute a recommendation to buy or sell any security. Past performance may not be indicative of future results. Any opinions stated are those of the author and not necessarily those of Raymond James. You should consult with a qualified professional prior to making any tax, legal, or investment decision.

Certified Financial Planner Board of Standards Inc. (CFP Board) owns the certification marks CFP®, CERTIFIED FINANCIAL PLANNER™, CFP® (with plaque design), and CFP® (with flame design) in the U.S., which it authorizes use of by individuals who successfully complete CFP Board's initial and ongoing certification requirements.

Published by River Grove Books
Austin, TX
www.rivergrovebooks.com

Distributed by River Grove Books

Design and composition by Greenleaf Book Group
Cover design by Greenleaf Book Group
Cover Images: ©iStockphoto.com/Andrey_KZ
and ©iStockphoto.com/petekarici

Publisher's Cataloging-in-Publication data is available.

Print ISBN: 978-1-63299-283-3

eBook ISBN: 978-1-63299-284-0

First Edition

For my mother, who once told me she had several books inside her that needed to be written. Little did she know that her tossed-off comment would be the catalyst that I, too, could write a book. Your turn, Mom.

CONTENTS

Watch Your Spending

Get Out of Debt

Simplify Your Saving and Investing

Simplify Money for Your Kids

Protect Your Family and Pay Your Taxes

Rethink Retirement and College

Bigger Moves

Conclusion

INTRODUCTION

This book has been in my heart for more than twenty years. Ever since I read Elaine St. James' book *Simplify Your Life* in 1996, I have been on a journey to simplify my life in every way possible. Perhaps I am a slow learner, but this has not been an easy journey. I am a highly ambitious, "Type A" hurricane of a person, so slowing down to simplify is a difficult work in progress. But my interest in minimalism and simple living has persisted.

The other big event for me in 1996 was starting my career as a financial planner. Right from the beginning, what I learned about simple living and minimalism informed my work with my financial planning clients. My goal was, and continues to be, to make my clients' financial lives as simple and stress-free as possible.

Ambitious, busy people can really accomplish a lot in their lives, but we also tend to be major procrastinators. In the time since I first decided to write a book about simplifying your financial life, technology has changed significantly. But most of the concepts I have written about here are nearly identical to what I would have written about twenty years ago if I had gotten my act together. Some of the applications of the ideas may have changed, but the ideas themselves are no different.

It was lovely to finally cross "write the damn book" off my yellowed, tattered to-do list, to be sure. But as I finally got started on this book, I realized that all this simplifying work is ongoing—a cyclical work in progress. That realization, coupled with my love of teaching and my desire to bring basic, no-nonsense financial education to everyday people, inspired me to start a whole new online business called SimpleMoney. (I did mention I am a Type A, right?)

SimpleMoney started as a blog and a podcast, and over time I plan to add coursework in the fundamentals of financial planning and simplifying your finances. There will also be other books, I feel sure.

For now, there is *this book*. This is a personal finance book like no other. It is not meant to be a comprehensive review of all areas of personal finance. It is meant to help you develop a new way of thinking about your money. Handling your money doesn't have to be hard. While there are complex things you can do with your money if you choose, being successful with your money can be very, very simple.

My aim with *Simplify Your Financial Life* is to offer you a new mindset about money, as well as practical tips to get your financial life under control. I want to eliminate the time you spend worrying about your finances, so you have more "white space" in your life to use as you wish.

The book is divided into twelve sections. We begin with some basics to set the tone and lay a solid foundation and then dive into building a better mindset about money. Activities, such as establishing a dedicated space to do your routine financial work, get you motivated and direct your focus. Changing your mindset around money is a tougher challenge. We spend years being fed ideas about our abilities and about how money works, so we should expect that changing those long-held beliefs will take time. Let's start now!

Next, we tackle organization. Being organized and focused is key to accelerating your financial success. Along with organization comes system building. The most effective way to simplify our financial lives is to build easy-to-remember, easy-to-implement systems. We'll discuss several strategies that do just that.

After we get moving on systems and organization, the book shifts to more topic-specific tips. Budgeting, spending, and getting out of debt feature prominently, but saving and investing are also covered. If you have children or grandchildren, you will enjoy the section about simplifying money for your kids. Starting kids off with a healthy relationship with money management is critical.

We wrap up with specific strategies for protecting your family, retirement planning, and college planning. The last section features bigger moves. These strategies will help those of you who want to make faster, more dramatic changes to your financial situation.

You can read the book straight through, if you'd like, but you can also pick and choose the subjects and chapters that appeal to you the most. If you want to implement the practices outlined here, you could choose to do one or two projects per week. There are 104 projects, so at a pace of two per week, you can transform your financial life over the course of one year. Or you could just choose the projects you need most and come back when you are ready for the rest.

My hope is that this book will stay with you for years, providing inspiration and a fresh view on your financial life whenever you need it. Remember, simplifying our *lives* is not a "one and done." It is a process and a lifestyle we choose to adopt going forward. Simplifying our *finances* is no different.

Start
with
the
Basics

1

SET A WEEKLY FINANCIAL DATE

It is sometimes tempting to avoid dealing with your finances (#6). Don't fall into that trap! Set aside some time on the calendar each week to address financial concerns. It's critical to make the time as sacred as any other appointment you might have on your calendar. It only takes a minute: Determine what time you can set aside each week to manage your financial affairs, and block out that time.

Establishing a routine is critical if you want to control your money, instead of your money controlling you. Repeating this financial work weekly will help you develop the habit of prioritizing money management. Whether you work alone or with your spouse or partner, building this time into your schedule is important.

How much time should you set aside? Don't worry about answering that one immediately. For the first few weeks, focus on developing the habit of spending time with your finances, and you'll develop a feel for the time required. If your finances have been neglected, your initial money dates might need to be lengthier. Eventually you will settle into a good groove. The goal is to fall into a routine that not only allows you to get your monthly bills handled, but also provides time to plan for the future and dream.

What happens on these money dates? Pour yourself your favorite beverage and settle into your rhythm. Paying bills or managing your bill-paying checklist (#31) should be a priority. It's good practice to review your retirement accounts or other investment accounts, as well as your cash cushion. Reviewing your budget is another task worthy of some time.

It won't be necessary to do all your financial tasks every week. Work with your financial docket (#33) to create a schedule for your financial management tasks, and then, during your money date, follow your plan.

Don't forget to make your financial date special! Play some nice music, drink some tea or wine, and use your favorite pens. I choose whimsical check designs when I reorder my checks because if I have to pay bills, it ought to be fun! Try to create a dedicated space for your tools and your work (#2), and then make it pleasant and enjoyable.

Whatever works for you, don't dread this weekly date with your money. Make it something special and enjoyable so that you will look forward to spending time improving your financial life.

2

CREATE A
DEDICATED SPACE

After establishing a weekly financial date for yourself (#1), identify a suitable place to work. If you have a home office, that's terrific. But an office is not necessary. Any place in your home where you feel comfortable will do! It might be at your dining room table, or on the couch in your living room.

It doesn't matter where you work, but begin to associate a specific place and a specific time with focusing on finances. If you choose a common space like your dining room table, you can't spread your financial papers, pens, calculator, and other tools all over the table permanently. Find a colorful binder, bin, or box that you can repurpose to hold your necessary tools. Store the box in a desk or closet until it's time for your weekly financial work.

Maximize your enjoyment and efficiency by having all the things you need readily at hand. If you are still sending bills via snail mail, for example, have your return address labels and postage stamps ready to use.

For my important financial work, I use a pretty purple

basket-patterned bin that my daughter gave me. While I have a desk in our den, I do most of my work at the dining room table. It is easy to carry the bin from the closet to the table and have everything I need handy. My bin is large enough to hold other work-related items, in addition to our financial papers, bills folder, and checkbooks.

The point is to make a system that works for you. Make managing your financial affairs a special and important weekly task. The more you dislike or fear working with your financial tasks, the more overboard you should go to make the time and place you work as special and fun as possible.

Life is too short to fill our time with horrible, dreaded tasks. Sometimes, however, we have necessary tasks that are not as fun as we'd like. Create an environment that brings a smile to your face, even when you're tackling something that feels challenging.

3

EDUCATE YOURSELF
ABOUT MONEY

You don't have to understand complex investment strategies and the intricacies of the economy in order to have a successful, simple financial life. But you can't stick your head in the sand, remain ignorant, and expect that all will be well. Fortunately, there is ample middle ground between those two extremes.

People have all sorts of reasons why they are unsuccessful financially. Maybe you were raised by financially irresponsible parents or were never taught about money. Or perhaps you consider yourself bad at math, and by extension, bad at money. Maybe you experienced a great financial hardship and essentially gave up on ever recovering from it.

Whatever your excuse for believing you don't play well with money, it is a cop-out. The basics of sound money management are not rocket science. Learning how to manage your money is well within the reach of anyone with the desire to learn.

Once you choose to embrace financial knowledge, where should you start? Master the basics first. Start by accepting that the most important thing to know about money is to *spend less than you earn, always.* Work on getting to the place where you are no longer outspending your income. A useful habit to develop is tracking all of your spending. When you know where every single dollar goes, you can better analyze and improve your financial position.

Next you can build on the basics in any area you choose. Learning about insurance, tax planning, estate planning, and investments are all good options. In addition, learn how to most efficiently save money for your financial (and life) goals, such as retirement and college tuition.

Along the way, remember two important things. First, *getting rich quickly doesn't work.* Real wealth building takes time, so be suspicious of any suggestion to the contrary. Second, *avoid the exotic.* Whether it is your investments, insurance, or any other financial area, proceed only when you have sufficiently mastered the basics. Stories are legion about people who follow a guru down the path of complicated stock trading or real estate investing, only to find themselves broke or massively in debt—all because they didn't really understand what they were doing.

Do yourself a favor and spend the necessary time to master the basics before embarking on advanced strategies. And remember: Simple strategies will get you where you want to go just fine. But it takes time.

Establish a Better Mindset and Money Philosophy

4

CREATE A
FINANCIAL MANTRA

I f managing money has always been a challenge for you, improving your mindset around your finances is a necessary early step. Start by using a mantra. A mantra is simply a phrase you create that can be uttered routinely to keep your thoughts moving in a positive direction.

For example, if you find yourself thinking (or saying aloud), "Money is too hard! I'll never understand it!" reframe the thought with one or more of these mantras:

I am perfectly capable of understanding how money works.

I can learn all I need to be financially successful.

On the other hand, if you find that you tend to dwell on your lack of money, try these:

We live in an abundant world. There is plenty of money for all of us.

I have all I need. I have more than I need.

Mantras work best when they use only positive language. They also work best if they are short and sweet; you want to memorize them quickly and say them to yourself repeatedly throughout the day. While you don't have to speak your mantras aloud, some people swear that vocalizing them is more effective than just whispering them or merely thinking the words.

If you are thinking this is a silly, worthless practice, I encourage you to try it before you discount the idea. I rolled my eyes at this concept until I used a mantra to get through a rigorous set of exams. Since then, I have been a staunch advocate for the power of managing your thoughts through the use of a mantra.

Commit to formulating and using a mantra for a few weeks and see if your frame of mind improves. Keeping your head in the game is imperative for financial success.

5

DETERMINE YOUR WHY

Being smart about your finances is hard. Really hard. Just consider all the temptations we face every day. Not only are there shiny objects we can purchase everywhere we look, we are bombarded with messages all day long about how wonderful our lives will be—if we spend our money on certain acquisitions.

Making meaningful changes of any sort requires work, persistence, and diligence. Sadly, there are no easy fixes. Money is no different. If we want more freedom and flexibility with our finances, we must take certain steps to get there, steps that require making some tough decisions and exercising discipline.

Changing your mindset about your money and taking the necessary steps to achieve your financial goals work best when you first determine your *why*.

How do you determine your *why*? Start by looking at your goals. Obscure, indefinite, and overly-broad goals never get you very far. Do you have a clear goal of where you want to be financially? If so, then take the next step forward and ask yourself, *"Why is this goal important to me?"*

When you have the answer, ask the question again, *"Why is THAT important to me?"* Ask this repeatedly to drill down to the essence of your goal.

Keep drilling until you've gotten to your core *why*. Only when you reach and identify the underlying emotions motivating you toward a goal will you realize the *essential why*. For example, earning more and saving for retirement might be your *goals*, but *security* or *peace of mind* is your *why*.

Keeping your *essential why* at the forefront of your thinking will give your goal the necessary gravity to make it a reality.

6

DON'T AVOID DEALING WITH YOUR FINANCES

I gnoring or procrastinating about dealing with life's unpleasant tasks is human nature. When it comes to your finances, however, this inattention only leads to more problems.

Does your paycheck fall short of meeting your monthly expenses? You might think leaning on your credit card temporarily is a good solution. And it might be if the shortfall is a one-time occurrence. But if you are routinely using credit to make ends meet, this is a red flag that your budget needs attention. No need to panic! Catching this situation early offers the best chance to stave off a downward financial spiral.

Another red flag is paying only minimums when you have credit card debt. Sometimes people pay only the minimums to avoid admitting they have overspent their means. Or they avoid paying more because they think paying the minimum is enough. This avoidance can lead to a twenty-year (or more!) payoff of what started as a small debt. And of course, the interest paid over the life of the debt will amount to two or more times the original charges.

Do not ignore collection calls! If you are overdue on any sort of bill, reach out and ask for help. Often a payment plan can be worked out with the creditor.

If your creditor is not helpful, consult your local Consumer Credit Counseling office, or other *non-profit* organization* whose mission it is to help with debt management. Be proactive and handle the problem when it first arises, instead of waiting until the situation hits crisis level.

When a financial problem starts to rear its head, your first thought is usually, "I'll handle it soon. No need to sound the alarm." Sometimes that is true. Other times, that line of thinking simply means you are in denial, and the problem is going to intensify before it gets better. It won't get any better without intervention.

Do yourself a favor and don't bury your head in the sand. Be brave and face your financial difficulties head-on. When it comes to your money, be the ox, not the ostrich. Strap on the yoke of your financial problem and pull that wagon with determination until you can lighten the load.

My advice is to avoid for-profit companies that offer debt consolidation services.

7

DEVELOP A "NEED VERSUS WANT" MENTALITY WHEN SHOPPING

You know the difference between wants and needs. Sometimes they change as our lives change. For example, mobile phones were definitely a "want" for prior generations. In today's society, however, smart phones have become more of a "need," helping us navigate daily life.

Wants and needs are very personal to you. For example, I would hardly consider nail polish to be a need (ever!) but someone else might consider it a very important part of their grooming. For them, nail polish is a need. You get the idea.

It's critical that you be totally honest with yourself. It is all too easy to ask yourself, "Is this a want or a need?" and answer with absolute passion that it is, indeed, something you NEED. But is it really? Brutal honesty and sincere reflection are required. When you think of something you want to purchase, ask yourself the requisite question. If you quickly answer that it is a need, check yourself with follow-up questions: "Is this REALLY a need?" and "Exactly what do I need this for?" Reflecting on these additional questions should do the trick.

Bring mindfulness to your purchasing. Instead of rolling merrily along while you're shopping, stop to consider mindfully what you need the item for. If you can give yourself the gift of stopping and reflecting, you might realize that you don't need as much as you thought you did.

And that means you will spend less money.

8

BE THANKFUL

D ay-to-day hassles are a part of life. Financial hassles are no exception. And feeling overwhelmed by what you're facing in the moment is part of the human condition. Those really challenging moments are the perfect opportunities, however, to catch yourself and pause. No matter how bad life and your financial situation may seem at this moment, stop and acknowledge that many people around the globe are struggling just to stay alive. We can always be grateful that things are not worse than they are.

Developing a gratitude practice is one of the most powerful tools at your disposal when you want to improve your financial life. Keeping a positive mindset is crucial to making progress toward financial (and other) goals, and being thankful is the way to get yourself back on the positive attitude bus.

My gratitude practice takes two forms. Every night as I turn off the light and snuggle down under the covers, I think about two or three things for which I'm grateful. I'm always grateful for my wonderful family. Sometimes my source of gratitude comes from more mundane things, like feeling thankful that I finally got a dreaded home project completed.

Stopping to focus on positive things from my day puts a smile on my face and helps me relax right into sleep. The experience is vastly different from those nights when I'm worrying about a dozen different things, or perhaps stewing about some rotten thing that happened during the day.

Which scenario do you think leads to more restful sleep?

The second way my gratitude practice helps me is on the days when everything seems to be going wrong. I'm in a crummy mood, something has me really ticked off, and I just want to quit or rip someone's head off. I have learned to catch myself in a black mood, stop short, and give myself a mini dressing-down. *Pull yourself together, Starksy, and focus on how damn lucky you are.*

Redirecting my thoughts to all the blessings I have in my life immediately shifts my mood for the better.

Figure out how you can include a gratitude practice in your daily life. Some people maintain a gratitude journal and faithfully write down three things each day for which they are grateful. Whether you write it down daily, think about it before sleep, or use it as a focus for a meditation, find a way to focus on your gratitude. You might feel grateful that you had enough money to buy groceries this week, or you remember a kind word that was said to you that day. Large or small, every aspect of life is a candidate for your gratitude.

9

BE GENEROUS

Along the road to financial simplicity and abundance, in addition to developing a gratitude practice (#8), strive to be a generous person. In your efforts to streamline your financial life, remember that many people have so much less than you.

Why is giving so important? Like creating a gratitude practice, regular giving helps you maintain the abundance mindset (#10) that is key to achieving success in your financial life. Maintain your focus on positive thoughts by being generous as well as grateful.

How can you help others along your journey? Financial help may not always be a possibility. The gift of your time, or of your service, will often be more valuable than a gift of money. Either will add to your sense of self-worth just as much as a monetary gift.

If you choose to give money, adding regular giving to your financial docket (#33) will make this easier. You can automate your financial giving to worthy organizations, just like any other auto-draft for paying bills. This way, your charity of choice benefits from your generosity throughout the year. This practice works well when you routinely give to the same organizations year after year.

Alternatively, you may enjoy spontaneous giving. Consider creating a budget category for giving so that you have funds set aside for organizations that inspire you each month.

However you choose to implement generosity, make it part of your daily life. Count your blessings and make provisions to be able to share your blessings with others.

10

HAVE AN
ABUNDANCE MINDSET

Maintaining a mindset of abundance is critical to financial success. Negative thought patterns sabotage most things we undertake as humans. To win sporting events, for example, you cannot allow room for negative thoughts. You must keep your mind focused and see yourself achieving your goal.

When it comes to simplifying or improving your financial life, the need for a positive mindset is no different and just as important. Well, maybe a little different. Of course, you can use positive thoughts, mantras, and visualization to envision yourself as a millionaire. But the importance of a positive mindset for your finances goes deeper. You must see yourself as capable, and you must develop an abundance mindset.

What is an abundance mindset? Thinking abundantly means acknowledging that there is plenty of wealth out there to go around. Finances don't have to be a win-lose proposition. When you are in a sales or competitive situation, realize that both parties can come out on top rather than one being a winner and one being a loser.

Thinking abundantly means lending a helping hand. Assisting others as they strive to improve their lives is a sure-fire way to spark the abundant mentality fire in yourself. Within reason, be generous with others (#9). That generosity will come back to you as you move along your path to abundance. Remember that being generous doesn't have to mean only giving money. It can mean giving time, a kind word, or a literal helping hand.

And thinking abundantly goes hand-in-hand with seeing yourself as capable. Feeling that you are capable of learning about money and improving your financial lot in life is the basis for moving forward. But you can't just feel it once! You will hit roadblocks and setbacks along the way, and it is important not to give up. Look how far you are now compared to a month or a year ago. How much do you know now that you didn't know then?

You are capable and deserving of an abundant life: a life rich with financial security, opportunities, and places to share your love. Remember that and be grateful for it each and every day.

DO THE WORK

A chieving financial simplicity and success requires developing the proper mindset. But don't kid yourself: You can't just think the thoughts and then go sit on the sofa with a magazine and a bag of chips. Achieving things in this world takes effort. Achieving *great* things in this world takes *great* effort. Simplifying and improving your financial life is no different.

It might seem counterintuitive. If you want to simplify your financial life, that should mean spending less time and effort on it, right? And bingo! That is, indeed, the goal. That's where you should aim, but you can't reach financial simplicity unless you set yourself up for success with some preparation. Simplifying other areas of your life, such as your busy schedule, may mean simply quitting certain activities or eliminating obligations.

If only you could make your bills go away by NOT paying them!

Arriving at a simpler financial life requires some front-end work, and that is what this book is all about. Just keep your eye on the prize. Work on your mindset, organize yourself, and declutter your financial life through small steps that will add up over time to greater ease and simplicity.

Remember that baby steps will get you there, even if it takes longer. When setbacks occur, learn from them and keep moving forward. Keep your eye on the goal, your head in the game, and DO THE WORK.

12

MARRY CAREFULLY

Choosing a life partner is an important decision. When you factor in financial considerations, the choice is even more challenging. *I'm NOT suggesting that you marry for money.* I am suggesting that you carefully consider money and the role it will play in your married life.

Before you marry, have honest communication with your partner about how each of you thinks about and uses money, as well as what sorts of assets and debts you have. If it takes paying a counselor to lead you through this conversation, that is money well spent. Nothing gets a new marriage off to a worse start than learning that your new spouse is up to his or her eyeballs in debt . . . after you've said your vows. Of course, I'm not suggesting that you never marry someone with debt, but you need to take a good, long look at the situation and develop a plan *together* to move forward with your money successfully as a couple.

Also, consider your partner's money personality. Opposites tend to attract, so there is a high probability that if you are a spender, you will be attracted to a saver, and vice versa. Again, this is not a problem. But it is a scenario where it's important to learn about each other so that you can work together on your financial life and avoid strife later.

Your mother probably told you, but I'll remind you again: You cannot change people. They must want to change themselves. Remember this as you approach the decision to marry, because in the haze of love and romance, it is easy to assume you will be able to influence your partner's behavior later. Open and honest communication from the start will go a long way toward preserving marital harmony later.

Above all, it is important to remember that you are now a team, so adjusting your mindset from self-preservation to teamwork is critical.

13

IT'S OKAY TO ASPIRE. JUST KEEP IT IN CHECK!

I am an enormous fan of big, juicy goals. It is difficult to improve your life if you don't have an objective to achieve. The trouble with goals occurs when people fail to reach them, and then give up on goal setting entirely, thinking it's impossible.

That is the wrong conclusion. Goals give us a target and get us started down the path to that target. Even if you don't achieve your goal, you will be farther down the path than if you'd had no goal to start with, right?

So, dream big when it comes to your finances. Aspire to make more income, get a better job, have a bigger house, or travel around the world. But keep those aspirations in check.

What does *keeping your aspirations in check* mean? Have big goals, but work from a place of security, and have a plan. First and foremost, have a solid financial foundation. Get the basics in place, including having a healthy emergency fund and ensuring your debt is under control.

Don't jeopardize your current financial security by leaping prematurely toward your higher aspirations. Instead, create a plan to get where you want to be. Taking things in stages is the best approach. A firm foundation will keep you and your family financially sound as you take the next steps on the path to your goals. Working from that place of security will help you avoid catastrophe if things do not go according to plan.

Slow and steady wins the race; that dictum holds most true when it comes to achieving big goals. Build a stable platform; then stretch to the next level. Once that level is achieved, solidify your new foundation and reach again.

14

BEWARE OF SUNK COSTS

I f you look around your house, you see things. Lots of things. Things you may no longer need, or things that no longer bring you any joy. You're certain that if you just had less stuff, you'd feel more relaxed and happier.

As you retrieve a box to declutter those past treasures, however, a strange phenomenon occurs that stops you dead in your tracks. An evil thought pops into your mind: "But I paid good money for that!" Thinking about how much money you shelled out for these no-longer-loved, no-longer-needed items causes immediate regret, followed by a wave of nausea or possibly depression.

You put the box down. And then you do something else to distract you from your misery.

This is the phenomenon of *sunk cost*. The good news is, once you understand the premise of sunk cost, you can conquer it. A sunk cost is past tense. You spent the money. You can't un-spend it. Whether you keep the item or donate it, *you already spent the money*.

You can look at your unneeded items, tell yourself it is a sunk cost, get over your internal conflict, donate the item, and move on. A healthier approach is to pause for a minute and recognize the cost of that item. Consider the amount of work you invested to earn the money to purchase whatever it is, and THEN proceed with moving it out of your life.

Acknowledging sunk cost isn't a license to be cavalier with your spending and subsequent decluttering. Instead, acknowledging sunk cost is how you overcome the inability to part with something based purely on the guilt you feel thinking about how much you spent on the item.

Acknowledge the cost. Reflect on it, and vow to do better. Then purge the item. The truth is, whether it sits on your shelf or someone else's, that money you spent is long gone.

15

SHOULD YOU ALWAYS
BUY HIGH QUALITY?

If you read books and blogs about minimalism and simple living, buying high-quality items is always emphasized. In general, I think this approach is the way to think about our purchases. Instead of mindlessly purchasing low-quality but inexpensive goods repeatedly, save up and buy things that will last.

But is it a universal truth that buying high quality is always the right answer? I would argue it isn't. Whether you should buy quality over quantity depends on circumstances. Sometimes it's not possible or desirable to adhere to the philosophy of always purchasing quality. Let's look at both sides of the argument.

The main premise behind spending more to buy high-quality items is that those items will last longer. Buying higher quality might also inspire you to maintain the item more carefully, given the amount you spent to acquire it. You might also buy fewer items if you go the high-quality route. Again, not all these tenets will always hold true, but they very well might in some cases.

On the other hand, there can be some significant downsides to always buying high-quality items. The obvious one is cost. Sometimes buying the higher-quality item will cost significantly more than the cheaper alternative. And sometimes our budget cannot handle that higher cost. You might then decide to wait until you CAN handle the cost before you buy the item, but what if you need it now? For example, what if you need nice clothes for your new job? If you can buy six lower-quality items that will get you through a workweek for the price of one or two higher-quality items, you might have to make that choice.

Think about the prospective purchase and, based on your current financial circumstances, determine if you should wait and buy better quality. It's not always the case that you should wait. Buying a less-expensive version is sometimes the best approach. Regardless, don't beat yourself up about this decision. Do what you can do and move forward. Later in life, your financial circumstances might allow you to spend more on better quality if that is important to you.

16

MONEY:
IT'S NOT GOOD
OR EVIL.
IT'S JUST A TOOL.

oney is a subject fraught with hang-ups for most
people. I will admit I'm not entirely immune
to them myself. We've all heard and often been
warned that "Money is evil" or "The love of money is the
root of all evil." The general assumption is that people with
money are bad, and thus, money is bad. Therefore, you
shouldn't strive for wealth, because why on Earth would you
want to go to the dark side?

I believe the vast majority of the people who hold opinions like these are people who don't have much in the way
of wealth. It is far easier to throw stones if you don't live in
a glass house, after all. But there's nothing inherently evil
about money if you think about it objectively. So, let's break
it down. What IS money, really?

At its simplest, money is a tool. Money is a contrived system for measuring value—the value of work and the value

of objects. Throughout history, different civilizations have created different forms of currency. Currency is merely a vehicle or means of transacting value.

Money as currency has meaning. It is worth something, simply because we all agree that it is worth something. Way back when, we might have agreed in our village that a chicken was "worth" 10 shells (or whatever the prevailing currency was). As civilizations got more and more sophisticated, entire systems of valuing objects and work evolved into what we use today. In modern times, our idea of "value" has become skewed. For some ridiculous reason, we have decided as a society that an hour of work as a mechanic is "worth" far less than an hour of "work" as a Hollywood socialite at a party.

Arguably, our system is less than perfect in the United States, but we aren't alone. If you have time, it's an interesting digression to compare the "worth" of things across different cultures. But back to the original question—Is money evil? I say no. Money is just a tool. Human beings have deemed it worth something, and it is humans who use the tool with good, or evil, intentions.

Let me just cut to the chase: If money is not evil, then why are rich people pretty uniformly loathed by the masses? There are countless examples of wealthy people who do wonderful things with their money. They fund charitable endeavors, they build businesses that employ people, and they help their communities, to name a few. But there are also the bad guys, people who have made their riches by scamming people out of their hard-earned money.

It's unclear why there is a pretty chronic dislike of people with money. If you agree with the basic concept that money is a tool that is a measure of value, and if as consumers we vote with our wallets, then the people who are "rich" are rich because we made them rich. Maybe they created a company that makes awesome products we love to use. Maybe they provided exceptional value in their area of expertise. Or maybe sometimes we just buy stupid stuff with our money, for no rational reason, and that makes someone else rich.

Personally, I find the way some people have made their money completely offensive. But instead of universally hating people who have truly earned their wealth, let's focus on the fact that in most circumstances, becoming wealthy boils down to two absolute requirements:

1. You must provide exceptional value to the world.

2. Once you provide value and earn money in exchange, you must spend less than you earn.

There you have it: the secret to building riches! Now let's keep going and find ways to have a life filled with abundance (#10). And if we can simplify our financial life along the way, so much the better.

17

DIAL BACK EXPECTATIONS TO SAVE MONEY

D ining out and entertainment are two areas that can quickly blow your budget. Retail therapy is often another big problem. If these budget busters sound familiar, adjust your mindset and commit yourself to a new plan of attack.

If entertainment and dining out are a priority for your family, discuss how you can re-engineer what constitutes a fun time or a good meal. Too often we default to the convenience of stopping at a restaurant for a meal. We can also indulge repeatedly in the same expensive form of entertainment without thinking about the costs. Taking your family out to a movie is a financial commitment these days! Sometimes just having a conversation about alternatives can remedy this sort of mindless spending.

The conversation you have with your family (or just with yourself!) should include acknowledging that if money is tight, recalibrating your expectations is in order. Perhaps it is just for a short period of time, or maybe it is more of a long-term solution. The reality is this: If your financial priorities are not being met, dial back the areas that are out of control.

And what about retail therapy? Retail therapy is a big problem in the United States. Some consumers consider it an idle pastime, while others have turned it into a full-contact sport! Shopping for fun—whether you call it window shopping or browsing—can be an expensive habit. The best solution is to replace it with an alternative habit. Consider taking a walk with a friend or browsing the local library instead. If you must shop, you might shift the direction of your shopping to yard sales and thrift stores. The adventure of the hunt will remain, with potentially less damage to your wallet.

Not exciting enough? Then treat yourself to a fancy coffee drink as your "reward" for a hard week. I'm not recommending total deprivation. Just stop the mindless spending. If you can replace the spend-fest that retail shopping can become with a smaller cash outlay (such as my coffee example), you can feel rewarded but not break the bank.

The first step toward changing these behaviors is *awareness*. Stop and consider *why* you spend money when you spend it. Once you acknowledge the *why*, you can find a better, less expensive alternative.

The added benefit of this "dialing back" process is it also simplifies your life. Avoiding the consumer treadmill and finding cost-free or low-cost ways to enjoy life are hallmarks of living the simple life.

18

SIMPLIFYING YOUR LIFE REQUIRES BALANCING TIME AND MONEY

There was a time in the not-so-distant past when I was completely and utterly enamored with the idea of *true* simple living—living simply and self-sufficiently. I pored over Helen and Scott Nearing's book *The Good Life*, and I studied edible landscaping and permaculture.

Self-sufficiency seemed like an incredibly important goal, and as a result, I taught myself how to knit and practiced sewing. I was also very keen on gardening. Then I pursued my interest in medicinal herbs all the way through a certificate program in herbal medicine. It was fascinating, challenging, and the polar opposite of my day job as a financial planner.

During this phase, I envisioned the day when we would have transformed our lives from suburbanites to homesteaders. I would be able to cut back or retire from my day job and live *the good life*. But in 2007, things shifted.

That year, two things happened—one, seemingly innocuous, and the other categorically epic. The epic event was that I found myself pregnant at age 38. Greg and I had only begun discussions about maybe starting a family at the start of that year. And the odds were slim given my "advanced maternal age." During my pregnancy, I was finishing herb school and working, so I was extremely busy. Between schoolwork, my day job, gardening, and reading up on how to have a baby and be a parent, every moment of every day was consumed.

The second thing that happened was our garden was puny that year, but it wasn't through neglect. I studied and examined all the possible reasons why it was suddenly underperforming. The following spring was even worse, so I had an expert diagnose the issue. The proximity of a black walnut tree was the likely culprit, and the expert said the entire garden needed to be moved.

The idea hit me like a ton of bricks. I was very pregnant by that spring, and I was not prepared to take on the back-breaking work of starting a garden over from scratch. I decided tailgate market produce would be fine for now, and I'd return to gardening in due time.

During the following transitional years, when I transformed from being a wannabe-homesteader to a working, homeschooling mother, I learned some hard truths about myself and about life. One truth was that while I enjoyed gardening and herbal medicine, it didn't mean I was adept at them or that I found them easy to do. Despite all my studying and serious efforts, I just wasn't that good at gardening and herbal medicine. I enjoyed it all immensely, but it was a struggle from start to finish.

But there were things I WAS good at, and still am: working as a financial planner, teaching, homeschooling, and being a kick-ass mom.

It's a difficult decision to let go of cherished occupations or avocations, especially when you have created an entire persona around them. Self-reflection is important, and sometimes that internal dialogue points us to some hard truths.

Initially, my attraction to the ideals of the simple life led me down a path that seemed straight and narrow: pare down your belongings, enjoy simple pleasures, be self-sufficient.

Now I realize the first two—paring down and enjoying simple pleasures—were in my wheelhouse, but pursuing self-sufficiency was not. I could double down and get back to gardening and self-sufficiency. But what would I have to sacrifice since there are, after all, only 24 hours in a day?

And that is the moral of the story: Time is money, and money is time. I was trying to use more time to achieve the simple life I craved. While the work toward self-sufficiency was rewarding, it was also time-consuming and exhausting. I realized if I applied myself to growing my financial planning career instead, I could trade less time for more money. That money then gave me the freedom to "buy time" to pursue the other aspects of my life that I not only enjoyed, but at which I excelled—mothering and homeschooling.

I cannot overemphasize the fact that everyone's minimalism or simple living journey is unique to them. I remind myself of that very truth all the time. Guilt sets in when I buy grocery produce or seldom mend my own clothes. I pay someone to help keep our house clean, so that I have extra hours in the month to write and be with my daughter.

For me, simple living is spending as much *time* as possible with my husband, Greg, and daughter, Rowan. That gift of time allows us to have great travel experiences, meaningful homeschooling activities with Rowan, the ability to enjoy the simple pleasures life has to offer, and the pursuit of moderation as a consumer. That means I spend some money to "buy" time.

Time is money. Money is time. If you are interested in having a simpler life, it is critical to strike the balance between time and money that is right for you and your family. Don't be afraid to embrace what works for you. It may not be your original vision of the simple life, but what matters is living life simply in a way that is satisfying to YOU.

Get
Organized

19

CONSOLIDATE
YOUR BANK ACCOUNTS

How many bank accounts do you have? There's no correct number of accounts to have. Some people like multiple checking and savings accounts in order to facilitate the organization of their financial lives. If that works for you, terrific. Other people want as few accounts as possible, which is also fine.

The important question is this: Do you have scattered banking relationships for no apparent reason? Perhaps you moved and set up an account with a local bank but kept your accounts open with your last bank. Do you use both? Do you segregate your spending from each account for a particular reason? If so, then great!

If not, then consider consolidating your bank accounts down to one or maybe two banks. Doing so will reduce the number of paper or electronic items you must deal with each month, as well as providing a quicker overview of your financial situation each month.

If you are an avid user of online banking and auto-drafts, this can often be a huge chore. You'll feel great after you complete this financial task, but it might require setting aside an entire afternoon to finish the job. The "rip off the Band-Aid" approach is to sit down and knock it out—go online to every bill you have that auto-drafts from your old account and update the information to reflect your new bank account.

If this seems overwhelming, make a list of all the bills that get auto-drafted and resolve to switch two per week. This is a more manageable task, and in a few weeks, all your drafts will be switched, and you can close the old account.

When closing bank accounts, especially those that have had auto-drafts associated with them, I recommend letting the account "rest" for a couple of months before closing it. You can leave a token amount in the account just in case you missed any drafts. Once you have seen two monthly statements with no activity, you can feel comfortable in closing out the account.

If you close out an account and you accidentally missed a vendor that drafts, the draft will bounce, and that vendor will be quick to contact you to get new bank information. Be careful with this approach, though. Some vendors charge hefty fees for missed payments, and they view it as your responsibility to update your information. Being proactive and updating your account information yourself is the best approach.

20

PAY YOUR BILLS
VIA AUTO-DRAFT
OR BILL-PAY

This idea might make you squirm at first, but later you will wonder how you lived without it. Take a few hours one weekend and make phone or online arrangements to set your checking account up to automatically pay recurring monthly bills.

Auto-draft is where you will set up the ability for a vendor to *pull* the money right out of your checking account on a designated day each month. Bill-pay, on the other hand, is where you arrange with your bank to *push* the payment out of your account to the vendor. Some people do not like the idea of a vendor having access to pluck money from your account. This is understandable, but I have been using auto-draft for many years and have not had a single issue with it. If you prefer to have more control, choose bill-pay.

Why would you do this? Having your recurring bills paid automatically will shorten the time it takes you to manage your household finances each month. Auto-draft or bill-pay can also help you avoid incurring late fees in the event you forget to pay a bill.

Be sure to note the log-in and password information you establish for each vendor, as well as the amount and date you have established for the bill to draft. Some bills are easy, because the amount doesn't change from month to month. Others vary from month to month. When those bills come in each month, be sure to mark down the amount that will be drafted so you can keep your checkbook register tidy and accurate. Beware of setting up auto-draft for accounts that feature a monthly payment that varies greatly, such as credit card statements.

Of course, there's a caveat to streamlining your life in this manner: You have to have money in your checking account for bills to auto-draft. Be sure you are leaving enough buffer in your account on an ongoing basis. You can also set up overdraft protection for your checking account, *just in case*. This usually connects your savings or money market account to your checking account, and if you overdraft your checking, funds will automatically be transferred to your checking account. You can also use a credit card as your auto-draft safety valve, but I wouldn't recommend it. Credit cards can get out of hand easily, and that is yet another money trail you'll need to follow.

21

SIGN UP FOR
BILL LEVELING

Bill leveling is the practice of setting up average monthly estimates and payments for consistency in billing. This idea most often applies to utility bills. The company looks at your prior twelve months of bills and creates an average monthly payment amount. The result is that your bill is the same every month, which makes it easier to budget and track.

Anything you can make consistent regarding your money is going to be helpful and will simplify your life. Putting your investments on auto-draft monthly (#67) helps you be consistent about saving. You can do the same with your insurance premiums (#85), but keep in mind that you will pay an extra fee for the convenience of spreading those premiums over the course of a year.

Even if a vendor doesn't offer bill leveling, you might be able to do it yourself. I had success once with a propane company. Since they didn't have a monthly leveling program, I simply computed how much we spent the prior year on propane, divided by twelve months, and then started a monthly bill-pay to the company in that amount. Many months the billing statement I would receive from them would show a credit balance, but it was later applied when we received propane delivery. At that point, the charge would net against the credit I had established. It might take a bit of effort to get the timing smoothed out, but it is worth it if it makes your budget tidy and easy.

22

BALANCE YOUR
ACCOUNTS MONTHLY

Sometimes I sound like a schoolmarm. But a schoolmarm is typically right about things! And balancing your accounts monthly is important.

Looking at the computer summary of your account is not enough. Use the statement that your bank provides, either hard copy or digital, and compare that to your records each month. You are checking to make sure that all your auto-drafts went according to schedule (and in the correct amount), that the checks you wrote and mailed were received and cashed, and that no unauthorized transactions occurred.

Some people distrust auto-drafts, thinking a vendor having the ability to draft from your account is risky. But I've very rarely experienced an auto-draft error. I don't worry because I balance my accounts every month, and I would quickly catch an error. If you do this balancing regularly, and you have been diligent to keep your check register current using your bill-paying checklist (#31), then this process takes an hour or less. The more accounts and transactions you have, the longer it will take.

The majority of the time, this is a rote exercise that feels tedious. But occasionally you catch an error (yours or the bank's), and it then hits home why this process is important.

When I was heading to college, my father told me repeatedly to make sure I balanced my checkbook with the monthly statement. Being the obedient child, I, of course, followed this advice to the letter, and still do. One time though, I was home from college, and my dad asked me if I could help him with a project. He had started bouncing checks. Clearly, there was an error in his account (because he was meticulous with his register); the project was to help him track it down.

Much to his chagrin and my eternal enjoyment, he pulled out a box, (a box!!) of a couple of years' worth of statements that he had not balanced. We hunkered down and spent an entire afternoon balancing his account. Fortunately, we found the error. Ironically, it was in the most recent month's statement, so it felt like a ton of work could have been avoided. Someone had fraudulently used my parents' debit card to make some charges, and that had over-drafted the account. Crisis solved, and the lesson was driven home to me again. Balance it monthly.

You can and should also apply this logic to your credit card statements. Review them monthly while your memory is fresh to ensure there aren't any fraudulent charges or other errors.

23

STOP RECEIVING
PAPER BILLS

I will admit up front, starting this practice was tough for me. I prefer having paper bills. But these days, you can choose to receive your bills electronically or on paper. If you want to streamline your bill-paying process, consider getting all your bills electronically. It will save you time as well as diminish the *Paper Monster* onslaught.

To aid in the transition away from paper bills, keep a list of all the bills that you are to receive electronically, and note the day of the month they are due. This will help you establish the habit of looking for those emails at the appropriate times of the month. This can be a part of your bill-paying checklist (#31).

One pitfall is the temptation to receive your bill via email, only to print it out for your records. More paper! If it absolutely helps you to manage your affairs, then do it. But try not to do it just out of habit.

Combining this with paying your bills via auto-draft or bill-pay (#20) is extra powerful. Just be sure to keep a careful checklist so that you don't miss any deadlines, and so you don't forget to deduct the amount you are paying from your checkbook register.

Another word of caution: Be sure to review the bill each month. Don't fall into the habit of just reviewing the amount owed and paying it. Some billing amounts have a way of creeping up. If the amount on the bill you receive is consistently the same, you're fine. But if the amount appears to change from month to month, be sure to investigate to find out why you're seeing variability or increases.

24

PRIORITIZE YOUR GOALS

I am a HUGE proponent of goal setting. But I have also had dozens of years of experience in setting up a long list of goals, only to feel frustrated and disappointed in myself when I don't accomplish them. This is both a universal commentary, as well as a financial simplicity observation.

With your finances, much can be gained by having laser-like focus. So while it is lovely and fine to make a laundry list of all your goals that are financially related, be sure to take that long list and prioritize.

Do you want a vacation home, extensive vacations, a solid retirement, and stress-free college funding for your kids, but you also have lots of debt and no real emergency cushion? It is fine to put your goals all down on paper. In fact, I encourage you to do so. Writing down and visualizing your goals is a first step to reaching them. But be realistic, and figure out what needs to happen first. In this example, building your emergency fund and getting consumer debts paid off must come before those long-term goals. Keep the longer-term list handy (and your dreams alive and well), but focus your attention on the most pressing one or two goals.

As you are approaching completion for one of your goals, queue up the next one. With money goals, don't rest on your laurels. If you have been diligently paying off a debt, be ready to redirect those funds to the next debt (or other goal) so that you don't get used to the extra cash flow.

25

CLEAN OUT YOUR WALLET

If your wallet is like mine, sometimes cleaning it out is more like an archeological dig than a simple tidy-up project. My wallet has several different sections, and I have organized it well. The prospect of getting a smaller wallet is out of the question.

The different sections within my wallet are routinely cluttered with old shopping lists and receipts. And don't forget loyalty cards and gift cards! With all this stuff, keeping my wallet organized is a challenge.

My solution is to simply purge the wallet from time to time. This gives me the opportunity to consider whether I need all those credit and loyalty cards and reminds me of the gift cards I have yet to use.

One space-saving idea is to use an app on your phone to store all the loyalty cards. I did this with an app called Key Ring. You simply scan in the barcode of the card and snap a picture of the front and back of the card, *just in case*. I was apprehensive about shredding all those cards, so I wrapped a rubber band around them and stuck them in a drawer. As it turns out, it has been more than a year now, and I am ready to shred all those cards. Eliminating ten to fifteen cards in your wallet offers up glorious space you can now use to store receipts!

I'm kidding! Regularly purge those receipts, too. If once a week you make a habit of pulling all the receipts out and dealing with them, your reward is a lighter, sleeker wallet. Be sure to file any receipts for returning an item or for tax purposes. Receipts for items with a warranty can be stapled right to the warranty information and filed. But more than likely, most of the receipts can go straight into the shredding bin.

26

DECLUTTER YOUR
BELONGINGS

A re you overwhelmed by your belongings? Is there clutter gathered in every corner of your house? How does decluttering your belongings help simplify your financial life? Clutter in one's life has wide-reaching effects. Physical clutter is associated with mental clutter, and when you are affected by stuff and needless thoughts, it is a sure bet that your financial life is also a cluttered mess.

Take a step away from thinking about your finances and instead focus on your space. There are many good resources for this project, such as Marie Kondo's *The Life-Changing Magic of Tidying Up*, or Joshua Becker's *Uncluttered* course. However you decide to tackle the project, the key is to simply start. Start small—clean out a junk drawer or clean out your car. Celebrate your progress!

While doing this physical decluttering, notice how that fog lurking in your brain starts to dissipate. By removing the clutter around you, you can start to simplify your inner life, too. It is all connected—your stuff, your mind, your schedule, *and your finances*.

As a side benefit, sell some of your belongings and apply the proceeds to one of your financial goals. Or donate the items and get a tax deduction for your donation.

One secret to success is to develop a minimalistic mindset about all areas of your life. Simplify, simplify, simplify! This will automatically bleed over into your finances and help you achieve your financial goals with less effort.

27

ELIMINATE CATALOGS
AND JUNK MAIL

C ontrolling the daily onslaught of paper is perhaps half the battle in simplifying your financial life. Changing over from paper billing to electronic billing (#23) and creating a simple filing system (#34) are great first steps in reducing paper that comes to visit you and then tries to move in. You can do more, however, to reduce the paper that comes in the mail. This project will take you only a few minutes, but the payoff is so worth it.

Eliminate junk mail. Visit the website for the Data & Marketing Association (DMA) either by searching for "DMA" or typing in this link: www.DMAChoice.org. You will find a ton of great information on this site and can register your household to avoid various types of junk mail.

Just how draconian you want to be in emptying your mailbox is your call. If you want to spend as little time as possible eliminating paper, register with DMA and call it done. DMA helps reduce catalogs, credit solicitations, and donation requests, but you can follow the next few tips to take things to the next level of paper reduction!

Eliminate catalogs. Visit the website for Catalog Choice either through a search or by typing in this link: www. CatalogChoice.org. Catalog Choice is a non-profit that is not associated with the mail marketing industry, so consider a small donation as a thank-you for helping fight paper waste in your life.

Both sites make a point of differentiating between *prospects* and *customers*. Registering with these sites will get your name off lists that are sold to companies wishing to expand their reach for new customers. If you are now, or have been in the past, a customer for a particular company, you will likely have to contact that company directly to get off its mailing list.

Why is this important? Because we all have a finite amount of mental energy to extend each day, and we need to use it efficiently. Time spent sorting through junk mail can only take away from time spent getting your financial house in order.

28

STOP PRESCREENED
CREDIT CARD AND
INSURANCE OFFERS

Are you ready to up your game on reducing unwanted paper? This project also takes only a few minutes but offers excellent rewards.

First, search for "stop credit card and insurance offers" in your browser. This will pull up a link to the Federal Trade Commission's *Consumer Information* page. You'll find a succinct description of your options on a single page. You can opt-out online for five years, or print out, sign, and submit a form to opt-out permanently from those annoying prescreened credit card and insurance offers.

If you elect to opt-out only for five years, add a note to your financial docket (#33) to remind yourself when you should update your preferences.

As with DMA and Catalog Choice, this opt-out method is not comprehensive. It does not stop offers from local merchants, alumni groups, or charitable organizations. It also will not prevent mailings from companies that consider you a customer. Those will have to be handled individually, and I'll share some pointers in the next tip.

You get a bonus for visiting the FTC's Consumer Information page when you scroll to very near the bottom and find a link for the *Do Not Call Registry*. The DNC Registry page is also an excellent source of information about those spam calls you receive, including which types of calls it is not able to block. You'll also find helpful information to get your phone numbers permanently registered for the DNC service.

Invest a small amount of time for a streamlined mailbox and fewer annoying sales calls.

29

NINJA-LEVEL TACTICS TO ELIMINATE JUNK MAIL

W ant to take elimination of unwanted paper to the next level? Try these quick fixes. They take only a few minutes, but they offer excellent payback for your efforts.

Do you regularly respond to mail solicitations generated by charitable organizations? If so, you can cut way down on the amount of paper you receive with a few modifications.

First, when responding to your favorite organizations, take a moment to write, "Please do not share my information" on the bill stub you return. While I don't have hard evidence that this works effectively, my personal experience has been a reduction in the number of related charitable solicitations I receive.

If you regularly support a specific charity and don't need a dozen reminders every year, write "Please mail me only one request per year, thanks." This has definitely worked for my family.

Place a sticky note reminder in the place you store your bills prior to paying them so you'll remember to write those notes on the stubs. Alternatively, upon opening the envelope, jot the note on the stub immediately if you intend to send them a check.

Another irritating interruption and waste of time is the sales call. Many people are compelled to donate in response to a phone "pitch" on behalf of an organization. For years, I have adopted the approach of telling ALL organizations that call, "Sorry, I do not accept any solicitations by phone. You are welcome to mail me your information."

They might follow through and mail the information and you can decide if you want to contribute or simply write, "Please remove me from your mailing list" and mail it back. If the phone solicitor asks for your address, say, "I'm sure you already have that information since you have my phone number." Don't be pressured into providing ANY personal information over the phone.

When it comes to the credit card, insurance, and other solicitations you receive in the mail after you have registered for the DMA, Catalog Choice, and Federal Trade Commission registries, simply open the envelope and write, "Please remove me from your mailing list" on the return stub. Pop that stub into the pre-paid postage envelope and add it to your outgoing mail pile.

If you are compelled to be militant about unwanted paper mailings, keep track of which organizations have gotten your instructions, and then if they do not follow your wishes, decide to no longer contribute to them. In the case of unsolicited credit and insurance offers, repeat offenders can be reported to the Federal Trade Commission.

I have not had to take extreme measures yet. The few charitable organizations that were sending me a ridiculous number of mailings were swift to adjust to once per year at my request. After registering with DMA and the Federal Trade Commission, I have also reduced many of those unwanted solicitations. They come so infrequently, I just chuck them into my shred bin and consider it done.

One last strategy is to manage the paper mail that comes from vendors you regularly use. For example, my credit card company sends me about a dozen offers each year for extra services. When that occurs, I write on the stub, "I do not wish to receive marketing solicitations from you," and that has solved the issue.

My approach has always been to lead with kindness: a pleasant "please" and "thank you" on my note, and sometimes even a smiley face. If they are a repeat offender, I add something like, "I have made this request previously. Please honor it." So far, I have not had to get ugly and report any organization for breaking the rules, and hopefully you won't, either.

Take a little time and apply these tactics to reduce the paper in your mailbox over time. Some mailings are queued up months in advance, so be patient. Offer a bit of grace, but stay on alert.

Your mailbox and our environment will thank you for simplifying your life in this way.

30

KEEP YOUR
IMPORTANT PAPERS
ORGANIZED AND SAFE

I f you were seriously injured or died today, who would step in to handle your financial affairs? A spouse or partner? Another family member? A trusted friend? Would your person of choice know where to find your various accounts and important paperwork? Even if you develop a simple filing system (#34), you want to keep your most important documents organized, safe, and handy for your loved ones.

The answer is to create and use a Document Locator. A Document Locator is a list, either on paper or electronically stored, to guide your beloveds to your important papers. In my house, I handle all the financial matters (a surprise, I'm sure!). If I got hit by a bus tomorrow, my husband, Greg, would be hard-pressed to know where to find all our important papers. You might be in the same boat. Moreover, everyone has a unique filing system, so saying "Everything you need is right there in our files" might be meager guidance.

A Document Locator includes categories such as insurance policies, investment and bank accounts, deeds, titles, wills, and marriage certificates. The sole purpose of this tool is to specify where a person can find these documents.

This tool may sound simple, or perhaps like overkill. However, creating this list naturally affords you the opportunity to gather similar documents and file/store them together. Since there's no magic formula regarding what financial documents should live where, the Document Locator simply explains where the documents can be located. You can feel free to organize your documents however it suits you. I have provided a sample Document Locator in the appendix, as well as a link to an electronic version if you prefer.

Keep your eye on the prize: Your loved ones will thank you if you leave them a locator that gives them quick access to important papers they might need if you aren't around.

Build
Simple
Systems

31

CREATE A CHECKLIST
FOR PAYING BILLS

C hecklists can be enormously helpful when you are
trying to simplify your life. Bill paying is one of those
tasks that can benefit from some structure and consistency. This is particularly important if you pay some of
your bills via auto-draft and some by mailing paper checks.

Create a list of all the bills you pay regularly, in the order
that they come due in the month. Each month when bill
paying time comes around, you can consult your list to enter
all the auto-draft payments into your register, and to write
out and mail checks where applicable.

If you want to up your game in this regard, you could
make a spreadsheet (a word processing document with a
table would also work) that lists the bills down a column and
the months across the top row. Each month you can mark
off the bills you are paying, either on your screen or via a
printout you make of your spreadsheet.

I have found that it also helps to include expenses that do
not occur monthly. Quarterly or semi-annual bills that need
to be paid are included on my sheet, and I just mark out the

months in which they are not paid. Whatever method you establish, make your checklist work for you. It simplifies the process if you take away the "Now, WHAT bills do I have to pay?" worry by keeping a list.

32

MARK IMPORTANT
FINANCIAL DATES ON
YOUR CALENDAR

I f you have a checklist (#31), you may find this unnecessary because you can use the checklist to keep track of financial deadlines. That said, don't hesitate to use your calendar to help you remember things like tax deadlines and due dates for important bills.

One of the best examples is management of your credit card payment deadlines. Penalties for late credit card payments can be severe, so monitoring closely when they are due definitely pays off. Certainly, automating the payments to go on time each month is one way to solve this problem, but if your balance varies each month and you like to manage how much you pay, you might choose to do this manually.

Some bills only come around once or twice a year, so those would be good candidates for marking on your calendar. Likewise, if you make charitable contributions regularly or contribute to an IRA or Roth IRA, those would be good things to note. Quarterly estimated taxes are another biggie.

If you use a paper or digital calendar, it is an easy matter to enter all those important due dates. The trick, however, is remembering to "re-load" your calendar after the date has passed. Moving the due date out a month, quarter, or year is key to being sure it doesn't get overlooked at the next deadline.

Alternatively, keep a simple list of these less frequent items (even if you don't keep a detailed list of all bills) and once a year, enter them all into your calendar. Don't pay out your hard-earned cash in penalties just because you were inattentive on due dates.

33

USE A FINANCIAL DOCKET

The primary objective of simplifying your financial life is to minimize the time necessary to manage your household finances. Think about all the other rewarding ways to spend your time! Of course, everyone's situation is different, but with diligent effort, you can organize and declutter your financial life so that managing all the moving pieces can be easily accomplished in a few hours per month.

A docket is a calendar of business items needing some sort of action. The financial docket is a great tool in organizing your financial life. It doesn't need to be complicated. Create a docket with a spreadsheet, a word-processing document, or just paper and pen. Brainstorm all your regular financial tasks and divide them into categories: weekly, monthly, quarterly, and annually. These recurring tasks could include paying bills, reconciling bank statements, reviewing savings goals, reallocating your portfolio, and reviewing your insurance coverage.

During your weekly financial date (#1), the docket will tell you what you need to do. No beating around the bush or moving papers around, trying to decide what is most important. Remember to include both tasks that you NEED to do and tasks that you WANT to do. For example, entering the auto-drafted bills into my checkbook register is a task I NEED to do to keep good records and avoid bouncing checks. But reorganizing my insurance policy information is something I WANT to do so I can better locate items when I need them.

Create an initial financial docket and work with it. You can add, shift around, and delete items as you go along. Don't be afraid to modify the docket to suit your family's needs.

Remember, the ultimate goal is to create an efficient tool that will help you get your financial matters organized and keep you on task. You'll have more time for activities you love.

34

SIMPLIFY YOUR FILES

W hile it seems heretical, I am an organized person, but I am anti-filing. No, I do not have stacks of paper all over my house. Papers are put into file folders. Filing takes precious time, and I discovered years ago that the time spent carefully creating a multiple-folder storage solution wasn't worth it to me. I found that when I needed to locate a document, it took me forever to remember how I had categorized that file.

I developed my own system and once considered it "filing for the lazy person." But I've reframed that negative thought. Now I consider the system an act of simple genius! It streamlines my filing efforts. Here is my system.

For personal financial papers (my businesses have their own files that are separate), I've designated three storage places in my house. My current folder, which I call my *Bills* file, is first. When bills come into the house, envelopes are opened, unnecessary marketing inserts are thrown right into the shred basket, and the items that need addressing are added to the *Bills* folder.

During my weekly financial date (#1), I tackle all the items in the *Bills* folder that need attention that week. Papers I am now finished with either get added to the shred bin or moved to the second paper place in my house: my *To File* file. Once upon a time, this file was my paper purgatory, storing papers that needed filing into my elaborate system of folders.

As I am a lazy, procrastinating filer, this folder fattened up quickly, making the prospect of filing all that paper more daunting. As a result, I just wouldn't file it. Finally, one day I just gave up on the elaborate filing system and kept everything in the *To File* file. I have continued to keep a *To File* file largely because it makes me laugh to tell my husband Greg to look for something in the *To File* file! Feel free to name your file something that makes sense for your system. My *To File* and *Bills* folders live in my desk drawer.

My financial docket (#33) reminds me three or four times a year to spend five minutes cleaning out the *To File* folder. Often, I keep bill stubs after the bill has been paid, as well as the monthly statement for my insurance auto-drafts, paycheck stubs, and utility statements. While I never intend to keep those items indefinitely, I let them live a while in the *To File* file and then shred them. My rationale is that sometimes I have needed to refer to one or more of these items within a few months, but never years later.

When I clean out this file folder a few times per year, I come across things that need to go into my semi-permanent or permanent storage, such as insurance policy renewal papers. I use a plastic accordion-style file organizer for this purpose. I have the tabs of the sections labeled, so in goes the current version, and out goes the older version. The organizer has separate sleeves but no folders. Avoiding folders keeps the bulk of the organizer to a minimum.

I use this accordion-style organizer because it is fairly sleek and has a handle, making it easy to grab if we're traveling in the RV for some length of time. Other things that live in there include actual insurance policies, passports, marriage and birth certificates, titles, and deeds.

Usually I purge my *To File* folder in February, so I can cull out all documents that apply to preparing my taxes. I could, of course, set up a separate *Taxes* folder each January and put tax-related items in it as the year progresses. But I don't want to have to think that much when new paper arrives.

Instead, tax-related items live in my *To File* folder until my February purge, when they get a new home in a file folder called *Taxes 20XX*, labeled for the applicable tax year. When my taxes are complete, that year's folder gets added to the second part of my longer-term storage system—a plastic file bin that lives in a closet. I call it my "archival" storage.

Voila! My lazy (or brilliant, depending on your point of view!) filing system. If a question comes up and I need a financial document, I can quickly determine where to look. *Is it a current issue I haven't dealt with yet?* Then it is in my *Bills* folder. *Is it something I've dealt with this year?* Then it is in my *To File* folder. *Is it tax related?* If I haven't prepared my taxes yet, it is in my *To File* folder. Otherwise, it is in that year's tax folder in my archive box. *Is it an important document (see appendix and #30) that I would keep semi-permanently or permanently?* Then it is in my accordion-file organizer. If the document is really old, it might be in my archival storage bin.

Free yourself from the constraints of dozens of file folders! Free up drawer space! Switch to lazy filing and simplify
your financial life.

35

PURGE THE
PAPER MONSTER ON A
QUARTERLY BASIS

E ven when you try to avoid excessive paper, life stubbornly remains full of it. While you might accumulate papers other than financial papers, the bulk of your paper stash will relate to your financial life—mortgage information, credit card statements, receipts, bills, and account statements, for example. How do you deal with all this paper? Going paperless whenever possible is the best idea.

Knowing what to keep and what to toss is more of a challenge. There are countless resources online that will give you guidelines on what is safe to eliminate from your files. The main thing is not to be a slave to a generic list. Instead, follow the procedure outlined below.

There are two main questions to ask yourself when thinking about the papers in your hands. First, do I need this document to prove anything, such as proof of purchase, proof of warranty, or proof of a tax-deduction. If you need it, then file it in a file designated for that purpose—taxes (filed by year), purchases, or warranties.

If you don't need the papers in your hand for proof of anything, ask yourself the next question: "How difficult would it be for me to get my hands on this information again, if ever I should need it?" Account statements are a great example. Most banks and investment firms now provide access to a couple of years' worth of statements online. If you need something older, they can provide a new copy of it (possibly for a small fee.) With these criteria in mind, you can toss the papers that could be relatively easily obtainable in the future. I always recommend shredding versus tossing paper that contains any identifiable information.

If the fear of chucking something really important paralyzes you, create a "Probably Don't Need" file. Tuck that file away in the corner of a closet and let one or two quarters go by. If you have not needed anything from the file, eliminate it! I promise you the vast majority of things that feel important to keep are totally unnecessary.

This process is relatively easy and fun because it's likely you'll see some gratifying progress straight away. Start whenever you wish, but the day you decide to take on this task, mark your calendar for three months ahead with "Paper Monster Purge" as your task. The initial time or two you purge might be challenging, but each time you repeat the task it will take less time, and you'll have visual proof of the Paper Monster's demise.

36

USE A PASSWORD
STORAGE APP

Make systems and automation your friends when simplifying your financial life. Setting up auto-drafts to speed up your bill paying (#20) requires creating logins and passwords. Keeping up with all those logins and passwords can be onerous. It can also be inconvenient. We've all been there. We've written them all in a notebook hidden at home, for example, and happen to be someplace else when we need to log in to an account.

Using a password storage app solves this problem for you. You create a master log-in and password to access the app, and the app keeps up with all your log-in and password information for all the websites you visit. Often the app also generates passwords for new accounts that are very difficult to crack.

Admittedly, I was slow to adopt this approach. It made me nervous to turn access to sensitive information such as passwords over to an app. But I did some research on different password storage companies, read reviews, and selected the one suited to my needs. If you frequently use multiple devices, it is important to find a password storage solution that will be compatible with all devices.

Setting up this system will take some time, but I can say from experience that the time it took me to set up and learn the app has been totally worth it. It has saved me precious minutes looking around for my password list or clicking "I forgot my password" and going through the ordeal of setting up a new password. In the past, when I'd get the new password, I always forgot to update my written password list with the new one, setting me up to repeat the process. With the app working for me, if I need or want to change a password, the app asks if I want to save this new password. Easy!

Schedule a time on your calendar to research, choose, and install a password storage app. As you access financial (and other) websites that require a log-in and password, the app will ask you if you want it to remember that information for you. You don't have to enter all your log-in and password data in one go, unless you really want to. Within a few months, you will have all of it stored, and you can breathe easier.

I will confess that I am "old school" and still maintain my paper list of passwords, but I find I need to use it less and less. Using a password storage app has helped simplify my life.

37

CREATE AN
EMAIL FOLDER FOR
FINANCIAL EMAILS

I f you are striving toward a paperless financial life, the trade-off is you now receive more email than you did previously. Fortunately, creating a system to keep your inbox tidier is easy.

In your email program, set up a folder for finance-related emails. Following my *Bills* paper folder example to hold all things paper until I've dealt with them (#34), I have named my email folder *Bills*. Each day when I am processing email in my inbox, I move anything related to bills or account statements I need to review into that folder. On my appointed day for dealing with my finances, I'll refer to this folder to get the amounts I need to enter into my check register for my auto-drafted bills.

You might consider more than one email folder so that you have one specifically for online receipts. I just stick everything in the *Bills* folder. It never gets too large, because once I've referenced what I need, I delete the respective emails. I keep receipts for some period of time, and if it is a receipt that is tax-deduction related, I print it for my tax file.

Create your system of email folders to best fit your style of financial management. But keep it as simple as you can!

Focus on
Your Budget

38

DECLUTTER YOUR BUDGET

A re you focusing on the difference between needs and wants (#7)? What about your focus on *meaning* as you make purchase decisions (#43)? Once you change your focus before you open your wallet, you will likely start to curb your impulse to spend. But you can also take a more drastic approach: Simply reduce your spending across the board.

While there are numerous ways to approach spending cuts, I like to treat it like any other decluttering project. This assumes that you already have a written budget, or at least a list of your monthly (and less frequent) expenses. Pull out your list and use a highlighter or pen to evaluate your expenses.

One by one, examine each expense. You can take the *KonMari* approach and ask yourself if that particular expense sparks joy in your life. Or you can try the *Your Money or Your Life* approach and examine if the expense is in line with your current values. Is the expense worth the life energy you are expending through your paid employment to pay for it?

Whatever method you use, don't rush through this process. Line by line, examine what you and your family are spending each month. *Slow down and bring mindfulness into the process.* Too often we spend on automatic pilot, whether it be on a whim at the shopping center or online, or through our ongoing monthly expenses.

I find it helpful to declutter our budget once a year. Many credit cards now have online reporting that allows you to see the categories of your spending. I find this to be particularly enlightening. While month by month you might think you don't spend much in a particular category, when you see how much you have spent over the past year, you might feel differently. We sure do! I also take the opportunity to review subscriptions and other monthly expenses that have become routine. I ask myself, "Is this still serving us? Is it in line with our family values?" If either answer is no, then out it goes.

Plan to declutter your expenses routinely. You will likely find expenses that can easily be eliminated, simply because they no longer serve your household in a meaningful way.

39

DON'T BUDGET. TRACK YOUR SPENDING INSTEAD

S tarting a budget is like starting a diet. It might be uplifting at first: It is exciting to take positive steps to improve your life, after all! But after a few days, you start to feel deprived and cranky.

My approach has always been to look at it differently.

The first thing to remember is that you cannot determine how to get to where you want to go if you do not know where you currently are. This also applies to your money. So instead of thinking you are going to start curbing your expenses with a budget, just commit to carefully tracking your expenses. Go about your regular spending, but meticulously track everything. After a few months you will have a much better understanding of where you are financially.

Parts of this project will be a piece of cake. Your regular monthly bills (rent/mortgage, electric, water, etc.) can be very easy to track. If you use a credit or debit card to pay for expenses, that can also be helpful in tracking your spending. Some credit cards even have online tools that will help categorize your expenses from month to month, which can speed up the process. When this task inevitably feels onerous, remind yourself that it is all in the name of science! You need good data to inform good decisions.

Tracking what you spend cash on can be more challenging. I suggest using a "Fritter Finder," (#44). Writing down everything you spend out of your wallet can be a drag, but it is tremendously informative. Cash is the easiest place to blow your budget, because once it is gone from your wallet, poof! It is out of your mind, just like that.

Another idea is to simply stop using cash and charge everything on a card that categorizes expenses for a few months. The caveat is that *you need to be 100 percent certain that you will pay off the balance each month.* Don't go into debt in the name of data collection! Using a debit card instead of a credit card is one way to avoid carrying a balance, since use of the debit card requires that funds be in the account first. Beware that debit cards don't provide as much protection as credit cards against fraudulent use.

Practice tracking for a few months—however long it takes you to capture all the things on which you spend your money. Don't forget the quarterly, semi-annual, or annual expenses when you create your list.

Once you have some solid historical data, go back and study your patterns. Find the areas that you think you can or should cut back to fund other goals. Then move forward with new awareness of where you need to pay close attention with your spending. This is your spending plan.

An unexpected side-benefit to this exercise is that simply *noticing* where you spend your money will help you control what you spend. If you must write down that third fancy coffee you are spending your hard-earned cash on this week, you are more likely to skip it. This simple step of tracking your expenses to understand your spending is subtle, but powerful. It might help to think of this as *ninja* budgeting.

40

ELIMINATE UNNEEDED SERVICES

This sounds pretty obvious, right? Usually, people imme-diately think of things like their gym membership when I mention this idea. Many people sign up for a gym with excellent intentions, but then their interest wanes. Mean-while, the gym keeps charging your credit card or drafting from your bank. If you aren't using your gym membership and have no immediate plans to do so, cancel it!

Many times, you can "pause" your membership without penalty. If you would like to resume using your member-ship in the future, but cannot use it right now, ask your gym about pausing your membership. If you paid in advance and want to cancel your membership, be sure to ask for a prorated refund for the unused time.

Of course, it is also possible that you won't be eligible for a refund, depending on the contract you signed at the beginning. It pays to be attentive at the outset of signing up for a gym membership, so you know what your options are. Most people, however, enter into a gym membership feeling enthusiastic at the beginning, and therefore do not think of things like, "What happens if I want to cancel my membership?"

This tip doesn't apply just to gym memberships. Take a good look at your credit card and bank statements each month. Do you recognize all the charges? In the world we live in, it is all too easy to click "subscribe" for a streaming service or other such subscription, and then only use it for a month or two. Scour your statements and then set aside some time to call the vendors and cancel those unused subscriptions. I always think I'm pretty on the ball about things like this, but I was shocked recently to find two such subscriptions that I had forgotten about.

Take the idea a bit further and spend some time reviewing other expenses that are on autopilot. If you have a landline phone, are you paying for bells and whistles that you do not need? Do you need the landline at all? What about extra charges on other utility bills? Are you paying extra with your mortgage payment for mortgage insurance? If you have been paying it for a while, and the equity in your home has climbed above 20%, call your bank and have them remove this charge from your monthly payment.

Conduct an audit of all the services you pay for, and honestly, ruthlessly ask the question, "Do I need this?" Chances are you'll gain by spending time online or on the phone to get those unneeded services cancelled or removed.

41

BUILD IN
SPLURGE MONEY

I n the *Focus on Meaning* tip (#43), I make the point that spending some money frivolously is not a crime. Ideally, life should include enjoyment and rewards. The danger comes when we go overboard, get into debt, and put ourselves into a bad position. The best approach is to bake some flexibility into your budget.

When your financial situation is dire, you have to curb any splurge spending. In those times, create rewards for yourself that do not cost money. A walk in the park, a hot bath, or an evening to yourself with a book or good television show can reward your hard work with the gift of time.

Once you are on better financial footing, however, up your game a bit. I recommend creating a budget category for fun, rewards, and splurges. It's important to make the amount you budget reasonable given your financial obligations. Even a small amount of money, if designated solely for splurges, can make a tremendous difference in your mindset when you are working hard to improve your life—financially and otherwise.

If you are interested in living a simpler life, small splurges can go a long way. Instead of spending your reward money on a fleeting treat such as a gourmet coffee drink, buy an inexpensive bunch of flowers that will brighten your day. Look for ways to leverage your splurge money for maximum impact, increasing your level of joy and contentment.

Also, as you simplify your life, consider what is important to you. Is your priority to add beauty to your surroundings? Or have experiences instead of more "stuff"? Perhaps your priority is to cultivate as much free time as you can as you move through your life. Keep in mind what's important to you, and use those insights as a guide in choosing meaningful splurges.

42

CHEAT ON
YOUR BUDGET

Not really. I'm not advocating you disregard your budget (or spending plan, as I prefer to view it). What I am advocating is to simplify *how* you budget, so that you will *continue* to budget. Keeping track of where all the money goes can be a very tedious operation. One way around this is to eliminate expenses or entire categories of expenses. If you spend your money on fewer things, there are fewer things to keep track of in your budget!

But life is messy and complicated, and often we have time periods where we have more expenses to keep up with than we would prefer. For these times, I offer you my solution: *a Cheater Budget.*

Divide up your budget into three main categories: fixed recurring expenses, variable recurring, and discretionary expenses. Your mortgage payment or rent, car payments, and insurance premiums, for example, are under fixed expenses. These monthly payments don't change or perhaps change only annually. These are also expenses that represent "needs," not "wants."

Variable recurring expenses might include your cell phone bill, utility bills, and cable bills. These expenses occur regularly, but the amount of the bill varies from month to month. While many "needs" may reside in this category, there are likely many "wants" as well.

Examples of discretionary expenses include groceries, dining out, and entertainment. This is the category with the "wants." Of course, eating is not optional—nutrition is a need. But eating out and grocery shopping are two of the biggest problems in people's budgets.

You decide what expenses belong to what category. So far, this is just like standard budgeting. But the cheater part is where the magic happens! Choose two to three expenses to focus on. Trying to manage and make better decisions about *all* of your budget items at one time is difficult and usually results in quitting. Instead, decide on only a few, and give them all your attention.

On a monthly basis, come up with a total dollar amount that covers the fixed and variable expenses on an average basis. For a ridiculously easy example, let's say you have $3,000 in expenses each month—$1,000 covers the fixed, $1,000 covers the variable on average, and $1,000 covers the discretionary. Let's also assume that the discretionary section is where you are focusing your attention. You know that $2,000 of your income is spoken for, but maybe you wish to decrease your discretionary spending from $1,000 to $800 to facilitate a saving goal.

Instead of dutifully tracking ALL your expenses each month, just give enough attention to the fixed and variable to make sure nothing goes awry, and only bother to track and notate the discretionary spending. *Instead of spending hours looking up all outflows of money this month, you are focusing on only a few areas.* Make a goal for each expense that you think is currently out of line. Then measure your progress each month against the target, recalibrating as needed.

Once you have reined in the spending in the areas you know are a problem, you can turn your enthusiasm toward other expenses in the fixed and variable categories. Can you cut services with your phone and other utility service providers to save money? Do you really, truly use your gym membership? Be honest with yourself, but treat this as a game that you can win.

By "cheating" with your budget and only focusing on a few categories, you will gain confidence and skills with budgeting. Once you develop the budgeting habit, you can expand your analysis to the remainder of your budget. Being a budget ninja should be everybody's goal!

Watch Your Spending

43

FOCUS ON MEANING TO EVALUATE SPENDING PATTERNS

L ike many human behaviors, when it comes to spending, we often get into ruts. We stop for coffee on the way to work, because that is what we have always done. Or we shop for clothes at the beginning of each season, because that is what we have always done. I bet if you thought about it for a moment or two, you could come up with many spending patterns you've developed over the years.

While I am a fan of automating much of your financial life (#20), I do not think we should automate to the point of abdicating responsibility. The beauty of automating our routine financial functions is that it gives us more time to conduct higher-level financial review and planning functions. Sounds like fun, right?

When we are in the thick of living our lives, we don't have the benefit of a high-level view. We're busy! We don't have time to ponder our decisions and weigh the pros and cons of a particular expenditure. But whether you automate financial functions or not, spend a bit of time in "review mode."

Look over your budget, a recent credit card or bank statement, or whatever documentation you can to review some of your spending decisions in the recent past. Think about each purchase and what motivated it. That quick donut stop last week? Were you genuinely hungry, or were you feeling sorry for yourself because you had a bad day? Those clothes you bought on a whim? Did you NEED them or were you just engaging in retail therapy?

The objective isn't to berate yourself for unnecessary purchases. The reason for this thoughtful review is to gain some insight into why you have the spending patterns you do. Once you understand your spending behavior, you can objectively evaluate whether you want to continue that pattern or not. It all comes back to mindfulness.

You will likely find, as I did, that you spend money in ways that most would agree are dumb or frivolous. But if the impact of the purchase is positive and strong for you, who cares what other people think? I often cite taking my daughter to Starbucks™ for breakfast when we head out for errands. I am fully aware of how others (or even I) might judge this habit. The food isn't healthy, everything is overpriced, I'm teaching my child a bad habit, and I'm demonstrating poor budget decisions. Did that about cover it?

But here's the thing. When I was young, my father used to wake me up on Saturday mornings and ask if I wanted to go with him to his office for a few hours. I always said yes, and we would stop for a yummy breakfast at a greasy diner on the way. This was my time with my dad, and the routine became very dear to me. When Rowan started coming to my office on occasion, I suggested stopping for breakfast at Starbucks on the way. The offer always motivated her to get out of bed and get going, and it became "our thing."

Spending some money frivolously is not a crime. If you are in dire financial straits, curbing ALL frivolous spending for a time might be required. Otherwise, don't be too hard on yourself. The wise approach is to have a solid handle on your budget so there is room to splurge on strictly unnecessary, but meaningful and desirable things (#43). Just make sure your frivolous spending is commensurate with your budget.

Ask yourself the question, "What does this purchase mean to me?" before you spend. By pausing to question your motives, you can insert a bit of evaluation in the transaction. If you realize you are just sad or lonely, can you think of a remedy that doesn't involve wasting money? Or if this expense is part of an experience that will provide lifetime memories (and you won't go broke paying for it), spend with confidence knowing that you are aligning your spending with what really matters to you.

44

USE A "FRITTER FINDER"

U sing cash to get through your week is an exercise in self-discipline. But even if you become adept at managing your money this way, you may still lack important data. If you are trying to follow a spending plan to understand how you are spending your money each month, using cash can be a challenge.

The solution for this is quite simple. Use a "Fritter Finder."* This can be an index card or small piece of paper that you keep in your wallet right next to your cash. You could also use an app on your phone if you prefer, but I recommend the tactile experience of writing it down. Every time you whip out your wallet to pay cash for something, jot it down. Whether you round off the figures or go with exact amounts is up to you. Gauge what level of accuracy is needed for your financial explorations.

Don't bother to categorize these expenses in real time. Just jot down the item or place you spent the cash, and the

---

*I always have used a plain index card for this project, but the credit for the name "Fritter Finder" goes to the fine folks at OnTrack Financial Education and Counseling in Asheville, North Carolina.

amount. At the end of the week, review your index card and total up expenses by the categories you are tracking in your spending plan. Focus on speed and ease to make sure you track your cash spending. Keep a pen or pencil in your wallet, or close by to facilitate getting the information down. You might prefer to keep the card and your pen in your car and jot down what you spent after you leave the store.

Feel like a dork doing this in the store? Who cares! People who scoff at your efforts are probably lousy with *their* money, so wave your nerd flag loud and proud!

45

SHOP WITH
A LIST

A ge-old wisdom, but perennially hard to do. How many times have you hit the grocery store for three or four items, but left with a cart full? Whether it is buying groceries, shopping for clothes, or especially hitting the big-box retailers, make a list and stick to it.

Whatever method you use to make your list, whether a traditional list on paper or on your smart phone, get in the healthy habit of using it. We have designated scraps of paper in our pantry to use for our grocery lists. When I notice we are low on cheese or eggs (or heaven forbid, wine), I add it to the list. My husband and daughter do the same. Then whoever is hitting the grocery store takes one last lap and asks, "Anything to add to the list?" and away we go.

Although you may arrive at the store with the best intentions, the siren song of advertising is strong, Young Jedi. If you walk into a store with wide eyes to scan for the handful of things you came for—plus anything that tickles your fancy—you are bound to overspend. It is human nature.

Never forget that marketing and advertising are both art and science. It is an entire field of study because it works. Advertisers know how to draw your attention. They know your hot buttons.

Traveling with a list, however, gives you an entirely different focus. Your shopping trip becomes a seek-and-find mission, rather than a scatter-shot free-for-all. I even approach department stores this way, but I will confess that I hate clothes shopping, so this comes easy for me. I make my list: black socks, dress pants, sweater. I have a mission. I'm not there to browse and see what I might like to wear, I have a defined mission to find the three things I actually need. This gives me the blinders I need to move around the store and avoid all the advertising temptation.

Is it a perfect solution? Definitely not. I am human, after all, and so are you. But I would bet that even if we add extras to our cart, we end up spending less shopping with a list than without one. The trick is to have a conversation with yourself about that extra item you are holding. Is it the sour cream that you neglected to put on the list, but actually need? Or is it a new brand of chips that you couldn't avoid because the display was smack in the middle of the aisle?

Incentivize yourself if that helps: "If I get through the entire store without adding non-list items to my cart, I will treat myself to a fancy coffee on the way out." This may sound like heresy and a sure-fire budget buster. But hear me out. If you make a thorough list and follow it, surely you saved more than the fancy coffee will cost, right? Make it a challenge, a game, or whatever will give you the motivation to stick to your list.

Be thoughtful with your list making, and then just follow your plan. Your wallet will thank you.

46

USE COUPONS,
IF YOU LIKE TO

On roughly four to six occasions in my life, I have been suddenly compelled to collect, manage, and actively use coupons. In each of those instances, I was in a place in life where money was tight, and I thought using coupons would help me save money.

Couponing, however, never caught on for me for any length of time, and I no longer even try. Occasionally some coupons come along that I might hold on to for a bit and even use, but overall, I no longer use coupons as an active technique for saving money.

I am certain that there are money gurus out there that swear by couponing, and to them, I gladly tip my hat and say, "To each, his own." Couponing doesn't work for me. I evaluated the time I was spending looking at the paper each week and clipping coupons, organizing them, and then trying to plan my meals and purchases to best utilize them. For me, the payoff wasn't worth the time and effort required. You might feel otherwise.

If couponing simplifies your life, or you just sincerely

love the thrill of the game, go for it. But if you don't, or you've determined that the investment of time and effort isn't worth it (don't forget your time IS worth something!), stop beating yourself up. Find other ways to economize, if that is your goal.

For me, religiously shopping with a list does far more for saving money at the grocery store (and other stores) than couponing ever did. Coupons are just another form of advertising, meant to capture your attention and encourage you to buy a particular brand. Often, coupons are intended to draw your attention to a product you normally would never purchase.

Simplifying your financial life looks different for each person. Be thoughtful about your patterns and habits and choose your battles. Don't add activities to your money management that won't bring positive results to your bottom line, especially after you factor in *all* costs—including your time.

47

ELIMINATE
SUBSCRIPTIONS

S tacks of magazines and newspapers are some of the
most creeping and insidious clutter. Chances are
they are hogging space on your desk, which takes
away your focus from managing your finances. And let's not
forget that subscriptions cost us money!

Take a hard look at what you subscribe to, both hard-
copy subscriptions and online subscriptions. Which ones do
you eagerly read each month when you receive them, and
which ones pile up unread?

You can take the draconian approach and just trash all
the piles, read or unread. Start fresh! Cancel all those subscriptions and move on with your life. Alternatively, cancel
them but retain the back issues you have yet to read and
resolve to read them within a short period of time.

I am not suggesting all subscriptions are worthless. The
ones that bring value to your life are the ones you should
keep, but don't waste your precious discretionary income on
reading material that just sits around gathering dust. Take
some time today to call or write each publication you aren't

actively reading to cancel the subscription and stop throwing money down the drain.

While you are at it, ask each one not to share your information and to remove you from their mailing list. This will prevent a continued stream of junk mail, snail or electronic, cluttering up your mailbox or inbox. It will also prevent new temptations to subscribe to something else.

48

CHOOSE LESS
EXPENSIVE HOBBIES

W ho doesn't love a great round of golf? Me, for starters. There is nothing wrong with golf, but it is my favorite example of an expensive hobby. If you are serious about trying to streamline your finances and make other goals possible, you might find cost savings when examining your favorite hobbies.

Some hobbies are inherently expensive, like golf. Not only does it cost a decent amount of money for your clubs and other equipment, but you pay good money every time you want to practice or play. Other hobbies may begin with a reasonable investment but the more you do it, the better you'll likely get. And the better you are, the more likely you are to start upgrading your stuff, leading to higher costs.

Think about how much you are willing to spend on your hobbies and proceed accordingly. If golf is your burning passion, then by all means go for it! If you are interested in pursuing a new hobby, think through the life cycle of that hobby and consider *all* the costs you will incur before taking the plunge.

In addition, stop and consider how you can reduce the cost of your current hobbies. Reading is a big hobby of mine, and buying books is one of the few ways I splurge with my money. However, if money was tight, would there be cheaper ways to indulge? You bet there would: I could utilize my public library more than I do. Our local library will fetch a book from virtually any public library in our entire state, and it is fast, too.

Another way I get my book fix (and could certainly do more often), is to frequent our local used bookstores. My daughter and I routinely take a box of books to trade for credit at the nearby used bookstore. We hand over our used books and have time to browse. And, of course, we take some more books home with us!

Buy used, borrow if you can, or simply choose hobbies and activities that won't break the bank.

49

PAY CASH

P aying with cash is probably the biggest step toward streamlining your financial life. Paying cash, instead of using credit, immediately creates the right kind of awareness about your spending patterns. Of course, it is complicated and probably unnecessary to entirely convert to cash. Having bills auto-drafted from your checking account is a convenience worth having when managing your finances. Since it comes out of the cash available in your account, it is an extension of the "pay cash" mentality.

Choosing to move through your daily life with cash instead of credit, however, can be transformative. Eliminating interest on debt is important, but more important is the mental shift that occurs when you stop managing your days with plastic. Credit cards are too easy. Hungry when you are out running errands? Just stop for a bite and whip out your plastic! Went to Target for two items you needed, and ended up with a cart full of things that you are now convinced you need? No problem, just charge it!

Eliminating the "spend now, pay later" mentality (#58) is important as an overall life philosophy shift. Paying cash is a good place to begin that shift since it addresses the daily grind, where it is all too easy to treat yourself after a bad day, even if you don't have any cash on you.

Carry cash and use only cash. The sure-fire methodology would be to leave your credit cards at home, but this may make you too uncomfortable. Either way, figure out how much you are willing to spend during the week, withdraw that amount of cash from the bank, and know it is all you have to spend. Do not resort to "Oh well, I spent it all, so now I'll just use my credit card." Switching to *cash only* provides some guard rails and develops self-discipline. When the cash is gone, you cannot spend any more that week.

If you want to get a firm grasp on where your money problems are, manage your affairs each day with cash. Give it a try!

50

REDUCE YOUR TRANSPORTATION COSTS

N ext to housing, transportation can be one of the biggest expenses in your budget. Whether you own a car or rely on public transportation, getting where you need to go on a daily basis can be costly. If you are trying to trim your budget or simplify your life, consider changes in the way you use transportation.

Spend a few minutes thinking about how you and your family use transportation. Use some questions as a jumping-off point to deeply explore your transportation consumption. Have you researched and considered all the different ways you might get from place to place? Do you use your vehicles sparingly, or do you drive somewhere every day? Do you and your partner (if you have one) have work-places that are in close proximity to each other? Do you have more vehicles than drivers in your household? If you use public transportation, have you explored all the various services available to you?

If your household prefers car ownership, consider the following ways to reduce your costs:

Buy less expensive cars. Forgo the fancy brands and do your homework. When choosing a car to buy, your main focus should be safety and cost-effectiveness, not style.

Buy used. Buying a new car with plans to keep it for a long time is fine, but buying a quality used car can be a budget-friendly choice. The key to buying used vehicles is to research and do your homework before you hit the car lots. Be sure to have a mechanic check the car over for issues a layman might not spot.

Keep your cars longer. Regardless of whether you go for a more expensive brand or not, aim to drive your car for at least seven to ten years before replacing it.

Maintain your vehicle. Give your car the routine mainte-nance it requires, and keep the car clean, inside and out. It is cheap and easy to get your oil changed on schedule. Regular maintenance extends the life of your vehicle, and it will reduce the necessity of repair bills later.

Consider if your household can get by with one car. For some families, this strategy makes sense and is relatively easy to deploy. For other families, switching to a one-car scenario can require ninja-like maneuvering of schedules. Unless you cannot afford to have more than one vehicle, think simplic-ity and convenience. If having only one car makes your life more complicated and frustrating, don't go that route.

Don't buy more car than you can afford. Not everyone can pay cash for a vehicle. If you need to borrow to buy a car, be very careful to evaluate the terms of the loan. Car dealerships now offer financing for five, six, or even more years. This is a mistake. Plan to finance a car that has payments that fit your budget for a three- or four-year maximum term. Buying a more expensive car and stretching the payments out longer—just because you can—is a mistake.

Batch your errands. If owning a car is a necessity, consider ways you can drive it less frequently. Batching your errands is one approach. Instead of hopping into the car for each errand, make all your errands happen during a single outing.

Work from home part of the time. If your employer is amenable, consider working from home one day per week. If your commute is lengthy, this will be a triple win: It will save you time in the car, as well as money on gasoline. It will also be better for the environment.

If your household doesn't typically own vehicles, or if you are contemplating alternatives to car ownership, consider these ways to reduce your transportation costs:

Carpool or utilize a ride-sharing arrangement. With Uber and Lyft (among others) on the scene now, there are numerous options to "rent a ride" when needed. And don't overlook carpooling opportunities. While it may seem old school, carpooling can make a great deal of sense if you live near coworkers or friends with a similar lifestyle as you.

Bicycle or walk more. Admittedly, this depends greatly on where you are located. People who live in the city will have an easier time implementing this tip. Biking or walking to your destination as often as possible is good for your health, as well as your pocketbook. For those in more rural areas, this might prove more challenging. If you must commute a longer distance, explore what options your local bus or train service might offer to accommodate your bicycle to use for shorter jaunts around town once you get there.

Like most things in life, the key to reducing your transportation costs is to increase your mindfulness. Study how you use transportation and think outside the box to identify alternatives that save you dollars and simplify your life.

51

FIND SIMPLE
WAYS TO INDULGE

O ne joyful step on the journey to simple living is recognizing and relishing the smallest, simplest life experiences. I think about a child's laugh, a beautiful sunset, and a playful pet as examples of what I mean. When we are watching our pennies, life can feel a bit restrictive. If we aren't careful, we stage a budget rebellion and spend a wad of cash in defiance.

To stave off that budget disaster, it helps to plan ahead with some inexpensive luxuries and special treats. This way, we can treat ourselves without breaking the bank. Here are a few of my favorite simple and inexpensive luxuries.

Plan a long soak in a bubble bath. Bath salts and other soothing additives can be very inexpensive. This is the sort of purchase I make when something is on clearance. Then I save it for just the right occasion. Bath products are often received as gifts, too, and those can be stored away for a time when you really need some TLC. Pour your beverage of choice, light a candle, and settle in for a long, luxurious soak.

Buy inexpensive flowers. I know this sounds like sacrilege. After all, most minimalists would say to save your money and spend it on higher-quality items. In general, I agree with that sentiment. But in our local grocery store, I can find natural, non-dyed flower arrangements for about $8.00. They easily last a week or more, and just having them on my counter makes me smile. They are such a pick-me-up, especially during the cold winter months.

Take a walk in the woods. Nothing puts your life and struggles into perspective like some quality time in nature. If the woods are not an option, find some natural place that means something to you and plan an afternoon of just "being." No agenda, nothing to spend money on, just sweet time alone or with your beloveds. I've never known a person who does this and comes home still grumpy or stressed.

Buy really, really good chocolate. If you are lucky like us, you have a terrific chocolate shop in your town (we have at least two!). If you don't, then most grocery stores sell a variety of fine chocolate. Buy a single truffle or chocolate bar and take your time to enjoy it. If chocolate isn't your thing, indulge in some other decadent sweet that makes you smile.

Spend a quiet night at home. Plan a quality night at home, either alone or with family. Light a fire or some candles, play some soft music, read a book, or play a game. Include whatever activities make your heart sing.

The magic behind these simple luxuries boils down to anticipation. Planning ahead allows you to get excited. Even if little to no money is spent, having a nice treat to look forward to makes all the difference.

On the other hand, you might also need a spur-of-the-moment treat to feel happy. Flowers and chocolate certainly fit the bill. In this case, make sure you have a bit of room in your budget for splurges (#41).

52

DON'T IGNORE
THE HIDDEN COST
OF YOUR STUFF

It's *sooooo* easy to buy things. Just whip out the wallet and pay cash or pull out the trusty credit card. Because buying "stuff" is such a piece of cake, we don't often have the level of mindfulness that we should when we make our purchases. Clearly if you are having difficulty making ends meet, mindfulness of how you are spending should be a priority. Even if you are not struggling financially, it is easy to fall into the trap of spending without thinking.

To make matters worse, often the *cost* of the item we purchase doesn't stop at the price tag we paid for it. There are other costs we can attribute to owning our stuff. It's an excellent practice to take our mindfulness about our purchasing habits to a new level—one that takes into consideration the complete lifetime cost of each item.

Items we buy need care over their lifetimes. Clothing, for example, needs laundering regularly (or dry cleaning!) but also possibly ironing and repair. Vehicles need routine maintenance and cleaning, and so do houses. Even smaller things need attention: Lamps need bulbs; alarm clocks need batteries.

Another cost of ownership that can add up over time is insurance. A new car will cost more to insure than an older car. What about the expensive jewelry you bought or the antiques or original artwork in your living room? Will you insure those?

When contemplating a major purchase such as a vehicle or home, or even a smaller, but valuable item like an engagement ring, do some homework to determine how much the insurance for that item would be. Obviously, you could elect NOT to insure things like jewelry; I'm not advocating for over-insuring. It is, however, a good practice to remember that insurance (if needed and desired) adds to the overall cost of the item.

Where will you store this new item in your life? Big purchases like cars or boats might require constructing a garage or carport to protect your investment from the elements. Other items might require a smaller, yet not inexpensive storage solution. Cameras, computers, and other electronic devices, for example, often require special cases to provide protection.

Take the storage concept a bit further and look at the cost for containers for all the additional possessions in your home. As things pile up, so does the temptation to purchase an organization solution. More bins, boxes, or cabinets will be just the thing to get us organized and help us store our stuff! While I have had those very thoughts in the past, my new reaction to the "I need a storage container" idea is to counter it with the challenge of determining what else to declutter to free up more space.

Last but not least, how much of your time will be involved in maintaining, insuring, storing, and organizing your purchases? In many cases, the answer is likely "not much at all." In other cases, however, a considerable time commitment may be a hidden cost.

Time is also a consideration when thinking about buying used versus new. Used items might be less expensive but may require a substantial time commitment to clean or upfit your purchase. This is not to imply that you should never purchase used items in need of repair or TLC. Rather, factor in the cost of your time if you are deciding between a new and used purchase.

Like most things in life, there is no right or wrong answer here. My intention is to encourage you to think about the lifetime cost of an item to help you be more discerning in your purchasing. Before pulling out your wallet, think about what additional costs might be in your future. Better yet, consider waiting to purchase until you can do some homework on what the associated costs could be before deciding to buy.

53

CREATE YOUR OWN
ESCROW ACCOUNT

I n most cases, when you have a mortgage through a
bank, the bank requires that you pay for your home
insurance and property taxes monthly. The bank wants
to be certain the asset on which they have a lien is insured
and in good standing with the local tax authorities. The
annual cost of the taxes and insurance is divided by twelve
months, and that amount is tacked on to your monthly
mortgage payment.

Accumulating funds for large expenses like property
taxes and insurance through the use of escrow is a handy
and less painful way to make the payment. Otherwise, you
would have to pay for the entire amount due all at one time.

The downside to using the bank's escrow service is you
are not earning interest on the escrowed funds while they
sit at the bank. If you are a good saver and your bank
allows it, consider creating your own escrow account in
an interest-bearing savings or money market account. Set
up automatic monthly transfers from your checking account
into the escrow account to keep yourself on track.

Once a mortgage is paid off, you will be responsible for your own taxes and insurance anyway, so using a DIY escrow account is helpful in accumulating those funds until they are due.

If you have other large, infrequent expenses such as long-term care insurance premiums or other property tax bills, use the escrow strategy to accumulate what you will need over the course of a year. Getting your timing right may take a while, since your various expenses may be due in different months. Nevertheless, building your escrow account over time is far less painful than trying to come up with needed funds on the fly.

A while back, I looked at all our family's expenses that crop up infrequently. In addition to the items mentioned above, I added our annual termite prevention treatment fee, the amount I estimated we might owe for taxes in April, and the estimated amount we need to pay for vehicle registration each year. I divided the total by twelve, and now automatically transfer that amount into our escrow account each month.

Escrowing needed funds takes the sting out of those infrequent, but necessary expenses. Smoothing out your financial obligations through ongoing escrow contributions can help simplify your financial life.

54

SIMPLIFY GIFT GIVING

T he holidays can be stressful on budgets, particularly since they always seem rushed and hurried. Of course, gift giving extends beyond the holiday season and includes minor holidays, such as St. Valentine's Day, birthdays, and anniversaries. Whatever the gift-giving occasion, simplify your life by having a plan.

Waiting until the last minute and buying gifts impulsively is how we are most likely to get into trouble. Although planning your gift giving ahead of time may seem as if you're taking all the joy and spontaneity out of the process, that is only partly true. It will definitely limit the time you'll spend wandering around stores in an effort to find that "perfect gift." But planning ahead also ensures our gift giving stays within the parameters of our budget.

The first step in simplifying gift giving is to make a list. Right before or right after the holiday season is an ideal time, because all your holiday gift recipients are fresh on your mind. To get a head start on the holidays, make a list of all your gift recipients. Include a notation of what gift you have in mind, as well as your target budget for each person.

If you compile your list after the holiday, include what gift(s) you gave as well as the approximate amount you spent on each person or gift. While you may not remember all the specifics, make your best effort to include as many details as you can.

If you make hand-crafted gifts for the holidays, note what sort of gifts you plan to make. After assembling all the necessary materials for your hand-made gifts, divide the total cost of the craft materials by the number of gifts made. Not only will your list be thorough, but you'll also have a record of what you've spent in previous years.

Using paper and pencil for this project is fine, but if you are handy with a spreadsheet, you can save yourself some time and effort. Spreadsheets can be set up to total your columns automatically, which makes your life easier. You can also just copy your prior-year list to get started on the list for next year.

Expand your list to include other gift-giving occasions throughout the year. Keeping yourself organized and bringing awareness to your spending is a win!

Gathering this data isn't an exercise in self-congratulations. If you have an overall gift budget for the holidays (and other times of the year), maintaining a list helps you stay on track. You may also decide to reduce your gift spending. Having a thorough list will help you find ways to economize.

You'll also be more thoughtful about the gifts you give. Instead of frantically shopping online or hitting the shopping mall, think about each person and what sort of gift he or she might like. When it comes time to shop (or craft, if you are making your gifts), you'll have laser-like focus and get your shopping done efficiently.

One additional benefit to maintaining a gift list is that you can annually evaluate who should remain on your list. Your child's teacher from last year, for example, might be replaced by this year's teacher.

At a minimum, evaluating your list each year curbs mindless or obligatory giving. It might spark conversation with family members or friends about alternative ways to celebrate birthdays and holidays without breaking the bank.

55

PLAN A SIMPLE, BUDGET-FRIENDLY VACATION

O ver the past few years, we have been RV travelers. As a family, experiencing new places by carrying our "home" with us has been a big eye-opener in many ways. The size of an RV dictates the amount of stuff we bring along, and that has taught us a lot about what we really need (and what we don't) to have a fun time.

RV traveling has also changed my attitude about vacation travel in general. Here are some lessons I have learned that have saved us money, simplified our travel, and helped us slow down and enjoy vacation more.

Research grocery options. Whether we are in the RV or staying at a rental or hotel, we find the nearest grocery store to stock up on food for quick meals or snacks. Eating at restaurants all day every day is expensive, and if you aren't careful, it can also be less healthy.

Call ahead to ask about amenities at your place of lodging. Many hotels provide coffee makers, and some also provide a refrigerator and microwave. If you are staying at a rental condominium or house, check what kitchen appliances are available. If you can eat some simple meals that you prepare yourself, it will reduce the cost of feeding your family and reduce the hustle and bustle of your vacation time.

Eat only one big meal per day. If the idea of grocery shopping and meal preparation is the opposite of "vacation" for you, then consider reducing your food costs in another way. Strive to eat only one large meal each day, and limit your other meals to smaller, lighter fare. This will not only keep your wallet happy, but your waistline will also be grateful.

Pack snacks. Buying food inside airports is outrageously expensive, and when you are out and about sightseeing, it is easy to fall prey to quick, but costly, snacks. We discovered if we bring a stash of protein bars and other healthy snacks, we can reduce the time spent seeking food in a new place, and save some money, too.

Seek out Happy Hour. Whether you enjoy adult beverages or not, many restaurants (especially in touristy towns) offer great discounts on food—and drinks—during the designated "Happy Hour." At home and on vacation, we often head to a restaurant for an early dinner to take advantage of deals such as half-priced appetizers. It's a treat for us to eat out, and we save money by not paying full price for meals.

Carry a water bottle. In addition to being terrible for the environment, repeated purchase of bottles of water can add up and put a serious dent in your budget. Instead, have each family member carry a refillable bottle. Airports and many hotels now offer bottle filling stations by their drinking fountains, which makes it easy to avoid the temptation of purchasing bottles. At a restaurant, you can order a glass of water and use it to refill your bottle before you leave.

Stick with one airline and hotel chain for loyalty rewards. If you are a frequent air and hotel traveler, you are aware of brand loyalty programs. While you might save the most money by always choosing a flight or hotel room based on lowest price and not brand, choosing one brand and earning reward points can simplify your life. I dislike getting emails from numerous hotel and car rental chains, and trying to keep up with multiple reward programs makes my head explode. This is one area where I choose simplicity over saving the most money possible.

Don't overload your days. When you're on vacation, it's tempting to fill every day with as much sightseeing and as many activities as possible. After all, you might never return to this place, so be sure not to miss anything! The trouble with that philosophy is that it is tiring, often expensive, and leads to overload. Which are you likely to remember more, the cathedral or museum you spent a leisurely three hours exploring, or the twenty-three tourist stops you made in two-days' time on a tour? Over all my years of traveling, the trips I remember the most are the ones that maintained a slower pace. Quality over quantity. Plus, you want to come home from vacation *rested*, not in need of another vacation to recover from your vacation!

Enjoy a Staycation. Sometimes the best vacations are the ones that require no planning or travel at all. Staying home and enjoying your own surroundings can be just the vacation you need. Remember you can also choose to be a tourist in your own town. Visit your local Chamber of Commerce to see what a visitor to your town might want to visit. Chances are you haven't seen all the sights in your own backyard.

Instead of falling into the same rut when it comes to planning your next vacation, think simple. How can you make small changes that save you money while also providing a slower, simpler, more memorable experience?

56

WAIT 30 DAYS
FOR BIG PURCHASES

We make our lives more complicated when we overspend. One of the main reasons we overspend is that it's so easy to do. If you are a credit card user (and who isn't?), spending is that much easier. Just swipe your plastic, or shop online. With just one "buy now" click, it's done.

But what if we could conjure up the ghosts of our ancestors, the ones who had to scrimp and save to make a big purchase? They understood delayed gratification because they had to.

Set a spending limit for yourself, perhaps $100, for example. Any purchase that would be over that amount must undergo a 30-day waiting period. Record those purchases you wish to make and date the entry. When 30 days have passed, you can reevaluate: Do you really still want that item? Can you afford it? If the answers to these questions are "yes," then go ahead and buy it.

My experience is setting up a 30-day waiting period can help you avoid impulsive purchases that you'll regret later. Whether you think about that item over the ensuing 30 days or not will be a big clue. Many items on your list will never enter your mind until the 30 days have passed. That's pretty good proof you really didn't need that wished-for item anyway!

57

EXPERIMENT WITH
"NO SPEND" PERIODS

A nother financial improvement exercise some people have utilized is experimenting with a period of not spending. If you are a chronic spender or a mindless spender, consider designating a week, a month, or even a year of no spending. Even if you are consistently adept with your budget, trying this experiment will teach you a lot about yourself.

Too often we fall into habitual spending—buying the same things at the grocery store week after week or consuming the same entertainment repeatedly. All of us have bought an item, certain we were out of it, only to find we actually had the product at home when you began putting groceries away. We don't take time to look at our inventory, and we are not always thoughtful about what items we really need.

A no-spend period puts the brakes on your spending in an innovative way. Simply telling yourself or your family members to "spend less" is ineffective because in the heat of a must-spend moment, the concept of spending less disappears. Consciously deciding not to spend at all, on the other hand, will make a challenge out of it.

First, decide how long your challenge will be. If you are terrible with impulsive spending, start with just one no-spend day, or choose one day per week not to spend. Your goal is to break the pattern of spending. Or dive right into a no-spend week. Once you have a week successfully under your belt, consider extending your no-spend campaign for a whole month or even longer.

Second, decide what your rules will be. You might avoid all spending except basic groceries, gas for your vehicle, and other necessary items (you'd want to be able to buy more toilet paper, right?). If you are going for a longer experiment, you might also exempt practical purchases you know are necessary in the future.

The key is to eliminate all unnecessary purchases. Remember, the point of the exercise is to stop all mindless spending and pay attention to what you and your family need, versus those things you just want.

When you complete your no-spend period, evaluate how you did. In which areas did you experience great success, and in which areas did you struggle? How do you adjust your normal spending going forward to address your problem spending?

Breaking your patterns, even temporarily, will provide you and your family with focus on the areas where you need to spend less. And less spending will lead to a simpler life.

Get Out
of Debt

58

STOP THE "BUY NOW, PAY LATER" TRAIN

Once upon a time, in a land far away, if a person wanted to buy something and they didn't have the money, *they had to save up to buy it!* Crazy idea, isn't it? Believe it or not, this short story is not a fairy tale. Ask your great-grandparents or your grandparents. Using credit for purchasing didn't come into being until 1950. My parents were toddlers then, so their generation, the Baby Boomers, grew up in a new world—a world where you could buy something today and essentially promise to pay for it later.

While the use of credit certainly can make life easier in some instances, it can also make life much, much more complicated. Used as a tool and paid off faithfully each month, credit cards can help you organize and simplify your financial life. The danger occurs when you neglect the regular pay-off.

It's a common mistake to "accidentally" slide into consumer debt. Perhaps you were paying the cards in full until

that one month when an unexpected expense happened. And then you carried a balance. If not remedied quickly, the slide can easily become steeper, until you are in a hole too deep for rescue.

I believe this is a mentality problem, not a money management problem. What must happen first is a shift in our mentality away from "spend now, pay later" and toward "save now, spend later." The added advantage to saving for items we want to buy is that it builds in "stall time." This allows you more time to evaluate if you really need that purchase after all.

Discipline yourself to set money aside each month for purchases, rather than buying on a whim. If this feels too daunting a task, start with just large purchases—those that cost $100 or more. Tell yourself that you will start setting aside $20 a week or $5 a day or whatever you choose to save up for that item. *(And you can repeat my mantra: Do I really need to buy this?)*

This one change in mentality can completely transform your relationship with debt. It can also absolutely simplify your financial life.

59

CONSOLIDATE YOUR CREDIT LINES

These days, every store you visit seems to offer you a line of credit as you're checking out. In addition to the major credit card issuers like Visa and Mastercard, many stores offer lines of credit specific to that store. Other merchants offer affinity cards with special offers like discounts at their location only if you sign up for a major credit card through them. And don't forget the "twelve months, same as cash" credit lines offered by some stores.

In other words, it's easy to accumulate a wallet full of credit cards. It is tempting, too, when the issuers offer discounts to entice you to use the card. On the surface, it seems you could take advantage of the discounts—so long as you are careful to follow the terms of each line of credit.

The trouble is, we don't. Most people don't pay credit cards or lines in full each month, and the credit issuers count on that. Even those zero-percent for X months deals are money makers for the credit companies. Sure, some people follow the plan to the letter and get to pay for their items over time with no interest cost. But more likely, consumers are

lured into spending more than they planned (or are financially able to) due to the "easy" repayment terms. One late payment can trigger all sorts of detrimental financial consequences, such as exorbitant interest rates that are retroactive.

A better, simpler plan is to resist the siren call of these credit lines. Is it really worth ten percent off your order today to open a new line of credit? That makes one more bill to pay, one more piece of paper to deal with each month, and one more opportunity to make a mistake and then pay dearly in the form of penalties and the highest interest rates.

I pick my battles on this front. A $60 purchase isn't worth a 10 percent savings of $6 if it means I have an extra bill to manage. But if the bill were $600? Saving $60 may make sense. In the event that I decide to strategically open a line of credit for a purchase, I will pay the bill in full the moment it arrives. And then I close that line of credit.

Managing credit lines boils down to time, diligence, and ability to pay. The important consideration is to know thyself. If you know you are less than awesome at paying things on time, don't complicate your financial life by adding more bills. If you are prone to overspend your means when the discount and/or low interest rate tempts you, just say no.

Sticking with as few lines of credit as possible is the simplest way to manage your financial affairs. Fewer lines of credit mean fewer due dates to juggle, fewer cardholder terms and conditions to learn and follow, and fewer opportunities to make a costly, time-consuming mistake.

60

PAY OFF YOUR DEBTS

Nothing simplifies your financial life more than living without debt. Psychologically, not being beholden to anyone financially is empowering. Being out of debt also decreases your stress level. But best of all, being out of debt opens up your options. You have far more latitude with both how you spend your time and what type of work you want to do.

If your first reaction is "easier said than done," I challenge you to think about this goal with serious, laser-like focus. Accept the fact that it may require years to accomplish. Be realistic when going into debt pay-off mode and don't think becoming debt-free will happen quickly. Otherwise, you'll give up when the process stretches on for years.

Laser focus is required. You must truly want to be debt-free, and your reason for wanting it—your WHY—needs to be big (#5). Maybe you want to retire, or you wish to quit a job you dislike in favor of work that feeds your soul. Or perhaps you want to have freedom to travel or spend time volunteering. Whatever your WHY is, keep it foremost in your mind as you develop your debt pay-off plan.

The first step in a debt pay-off plan is to *stop the bleeding*. If you are using credit for your regular monthly expenses, switch to cash. Or use a credit card that has no balance and pay it off in full each month. Your goal is to freeze your current amount of debt and not add a single penny to it.

Next, employ the "snowball" or "avalanche" approach, and put your debts in order for the most efficient and effective payoff. With the snowball technique, order your debts from smallest balance to largest. The strategy is to get some quick early wins by knocking out some smaller balances. You will be motivated to march ahead. With the avalanche technique, order your debts from highest interest rate to lowest. This approach tackles the most expensive debts first so that you pay the least interest while reaching your goal.

I recommend a hybrid of the two approaches. Having some early success by paying off some small debts has merit. But also take a good look at the interest rates charged by your debts and pay off the highest rate debt as soon as possible.

However you organize your pay-off structure, the process is the same: The first debt on the list gets the laser focus. You pay the minimum required payment on ALL debts except this first one. Whatever extra you can squeeze from your budget, tack it on to your monthly payment on that first debt. When that debt is gone, you roll (or snowball) the entire amount you were paying on that first debt and add it to the minimum payment you have been paying on the next debt on the list.

A couple of notes on this technique are in order. Don't add extra principal payment to several debts to pay them off faster. This sprinkling around not only dilutes the effectiveness of your efforts, but it also extends the time it will take to reach your ultimate goals. Remember, laser focus. Keep your laser focused on the first debt until it is demolished. Then shift your focus to the next target.

Secondly, regardless of the interest rate, put your mortgage last on the payoff list. Although you may hate the idea of paying for a mortgage for thirty years, do not be tempted to throw some extra cash toward the principal each month. Resist the urge to do this and trust that this system works. ALL the extra goes to debt number one on the list. As you knock out debts, the snowball amount you add on to the next debt will grow and grow. By the time you are ready to tackle your mortgage, you might have an impressively large amount of extra principal payment to apply.

Once your debts are fully paid off, resolve to stay out of debt. While there might be future times that debt is needed to accomplish some goal—such as moving to a new house or starting a business—go into high alert, re-focus your laser, and pay off the debt as quickly as you can.

A debt-free life is a simpler life.

61

PAY OFF
YOUR MORTGAGE

Remember my prior tip about paying off your debts (#60)? In case you interpreted "leave your mortgage until last" as a license to maintain it indefinitely, let me share some more thoughts about mortgages.

Often people categorize mortgages as "good debt." This rationale usually starts with the fact that mortgage interest is deductible. If I had a dollar for every time someone told me they didn't want to pay off their mortgage because it was a good tax break, I'd be a rich lady on a tropical island somewhere. There are no *good* debts. BAD debts (egregiously high interest rate debts, for instance) exist unfortunately, but being in any type of debt is not an ideal situation.

It's true that debt is used by businesses to leverage growth. Leverage is what you are doing when you use a mortgage to buy a house. Leverage means you use a small amount of money out of pocket (your down payment) to buy a large asset by borrowing. Using debt is not necessarily a bad practice; it is frequently a *necessary* practice. In business, strategic decision making often means avoiding tying up your capital by using short-term borrowing.

The key is to use debt as a tool, not as a crutch. Saving up enough money to buy a home could take decades, and meanwhile the price of homes would rise. Using a mortgage to buy a home makes sense, as long as you do it wisely.

Avoid following the destructive adage to "buy as much house as you can afford." I am not sure who first circulated that advice, but I bet it was a financial institution. Maximizing the mortgage for which you are eligible is dangerous, pushing your mortgage expense to the limit of what you can afford on your current income.

The theory is that your income will rise over time while your mortgage payment remains fixed, so a few years of struggling is worth getting more house. What nonsense. If we have learned nothing else over the past two decades, it is that incomes do NOT always rise, and job security is not a given. A better idea is to choose a house requiring the smallest mortgage possible. Or at least pick a mortgage payment amount in a range that is very manageable, with lots of wiggle room.

The reason I recommend leaving the mortgage until last on your debt payoff strategy is three-fold. Your mortgage is likely your largest debt balance. If you leave other debts unpaid until the mortgage is paid off, you might have gray hair by then. Secondly, mortgages have lower interest rates than consumer debt like credit cards and car loans. Lastly, leaving the mortgage until last allows your monthly payment snowball to be as large as possible, making the speed of the mortgage payoff pretty impressive.

But what about that mortgage interest deduction? Isn't that good to have? If you itemize your deductions, being able to deduct your mortgage interest is a help. The fallacy is to think it is a dollar-for-dollar savings, and it isn't. Let's look at a simplified example. A $250,000 mortgage at a 4 percent rate would cost $10,000 in interest each year. If your tax bracket is 20 percent, then you would save $2,000 on your taxes, bringing the cost of your mortgage that year down to $8,000. Your effective interest rate on that mortgage is now 3.2 percent instead of 4 percent. But you're still paying $8,000 each year to use the bank's money.

If having a mortgage is a necessity, then hooray to have a bit of savings via the tax deduction. But the mortgage interest is not zeroed out by the deduction. It is merely reduced. Why on earth would you continue to spend $10,000 each year to save $2,000 in taxes?

I'll repeat: A debt-free life is a simpler life. Be focused and disciplined. You can get there.

62

GAMIFY YOUR
DEBT REDUCTION

P aying down your debts can be a difficult and depressing activity. It can also feel overwhelming! If the prospect of being debt-free doesn't set your motivation on fire, or if you simply get bogged down in the process and find your enthusiasm waning, don't give up— make a game of it!

If your debt pay-down program involves your partner and/or kids, create a monthly challenge with each other to find ways to trim more expenses each month to accelerate your debt payoff. If you are flying solo, challenge yourself! Or find a like-minded friend or partner in crime who wants to achieve the same goal and do it together.

Regardless of who is involved, choose an inspiring reward. A reward that doesn't cost money is optimal, but if a bigger reward is required and desired, don't hesitate. If you are sacrificing monthly to redirect income toward debts, consider segregating a small amount into a special savings account to fund your reward. For example, if you are scrimping on expenses to carve out $250 per month toward your debts, put $225 toward the debts and add $25 to your reward account.

On the surface, this might seem counterintuitive. After all, putting every dime of spare income toward debt elimination would be better! But human nature being what it is, too much austerity often leads to falling off the wagon. By planning the reward ahead of time, you will maintain your enthusiasm.

One caution is worth noting. Make the reward commensurate with the level of effort you must expend to achieve your goal. Don't set aside more than 10 percent of your monthly debt pay-down for reward. Better yet, make it less than 5 percent, and devise a reward that is mostly non-financial.

If you aren't in need of a reward for motivation, maybe your game is to see how fast you can pay off those debts. Compute how long you expect your debt pay-down project to take, and then work hard to shave off months and even years to reach your goal. The faster the debts get paid, the less interest you will pay on those debts. And that, in and of itself, is a pretty darn good reward.

63

PROTECT
YOUR CREDIT

B eing responsible with credit is critical. Carelessness with payment deadlines and piling up credit balances will negatively impact your credit score and your ability to obtain loans at a good rate in the future.

These days, being diligent with your own credit is not enough. Now we must be careful that *other* people are not abusing our credit lines. You could "wait and see if anything bad happens" regarding your credit, but consider two other strategies. While in the short run, these strategies won't simplify your life, you'll be setting up ongoing maintenance now to avoid a major headache later.

The first strategy is delegation. Subscribe to a credit monitoring service that will alert you to suspicious activity. Some credit card companies offer a free monitoring service, but scrutinize just how thoroughly they are monitoring. Generally, a comprehensive monitoring system requires an annual fee. This service might include some financial reimbursement in the event you experience a security breach on their watch.

The second strategy is free, but it requires your consistent input to be most successful. Each of the three main credit bureaus (Equifax, TransUnion, and Experian) will provide a free credit report to you annually. Make your request at www.annualcreditreport.com, which is a federally authorized source for your credit data.

Mark your calendar and request all three bureau reports at once. Or for extra protection, stagger your effort and request one bureau report every four months on a rotation. If you are careful and mark your calendar, or better yet, make this part of your financial docket (#33), you can get in the groove of monitoring your credit for free three times each year.

Is three times per year overkill? Perhaps, but early detection of irregularities is key to reducing the stress and effort required to address the fallout from a credit breach.

What, exactly, are you are monitoring on these reports? The best approach is to carefully review the report each time you pull it to look for errors and unauthorized credit. Sometimes the credit bureaus will include inaccurate information (name spelling, wrong addresses, etc.).

The first time you review your reports, it will take time and effort to correct the mistakes you find. Going forward, however, you will know exactly what is supposed to be on your report, and thus breaches will be easier to spot.

Simplify Your Saving and Investing

64

PAY
YOURSELF
FIRST

Most people approach money in a familiar pattern: Get my paycheck, pay all my bills, and then if there is anything left over, give some to charity, and save the rest.

This approach is entirely wrong. With this mindset, you can never achieve wealth. Instead, adopt this pattern: Get my paycheck, set aside a predetermined amount for saving or investing, give some to charity, and then pay my bills. I know this sounds like lunacy. What if there isn't enough to pay the bills?

But the key is in the secret sauce. The secret sauce is your budget. If you know how much you require each month to cover your expenses (the required ones), and you know how much income you have coming in, you can assess how much is potentially available for giving and saving.

If you add up all your expenses and there IS no money left for saving and giving, then go back and cut expenses.

Once you understand what is possible for saving, commit to a plan. From that point forward, each month when you get paid, set aside the predetermined amount into your savings or investments.

You must do the spending examination (aka your budget) first to gauge where you stand. Otherwise, you may pay yourself an arbitrary amount. If that amount is too large and your budget blows up, you're likely to get discouraged and quit. That is not helpful. Budget first, then once you know it is possible to carve $100 per month (or whatever the amount is) from your monthly income for investing, set it up and DO IT.

What if your bills are higher and after you invest, you don't have enough to cover your bills? It's up to you: Put on your big-kid pants and curb your spending. You can always curb discretionary spending in order to maintain your savings and investing pattern.

If you don't prioritize yourself and your family in this scenario, you will never get ahead. Remember on the plane how you need to put on your own oxygen mask before helping others? That applies here, too. Prioritize building your wealth before allowing yourself the freedom to blow that money elsewhere.

65

BUILD AN
EMERGENCY FUND

E mergency funds help you through life's unexpected twists. Conventional wisdom suggests that you accumulate a fund that is equal to three to six months of your living expenses. Let's say you need $3,000 per month to meet all your expenses. Your target emergency fund should then be $9,000 to $18,000.

You may think this is a staggering amount of money to save up for that rainy day, and you would not be alone. Many people get this far in the process (calculating what their fund should be), and they immediately throw in the towel. It feels like an impossible task.

The solution? Just chuck that three- to six-month requirement right out the window. Start small. Take baby steps toward your goal. Aim to build a savings of $1,000 first. And if that feels too big, use $500 as your target. Still too daunting? Make it $100. Find a number that requires a bit of effort on your part, but isn't so overwhelming that it makes you want to cry. Set the target, and then go open a savings or money market account where you bank and get started.

When you hit your first target, give yourself a big pat on the back. Then ratchet up that goal. Have your $100? Now build it to $200. Got to your $500? Now reset the target to $1,000. Don't make the mistake of thinking, "Oh, I reached my goal, and now I'll just keep building it." While that approach might seem natural and workable, psychologically it is likely to fail. Always define your target. Your brain works better at reaching for and achieving goals if the goal is well-defined.

Regardless of the scale of your continual increases, hit your target, then ratchet it up and keep working. Celebrate your victories along the way, but not by spending your emergency fund! Eventually your savings will grow, the *habit* of saving will grow, and before you know it, you will have accumulated that magical three to six months' emergency fund.

66

SLOW AND STEADY
WINS THE RACE

I t only takes a few minutes to search on the internet and
find some program that will make you rich quickly. At
least, that is the claim. Sure, there are people out there
who have had some lucky set of circumstances handed to
them, allowing them to leverage one advantage into great
wealth. But I would argue that no one gets wealthy without
hard work. Or at least, no one deserves to!

Since I am a complete "negative Nellie" when it comes
to quick enrichment schemes, I focus on what DOES work—
consistent investing over the long haul. Being a successful
investor and building wealth require discipline and patience.

First you must build the discipline to pay yourself first
(#64). Build up an emergency cushion that is appropriate
and comfortable for you (#65). Once that is established
and your consumer debt is under control, turn your attention to investments.

The main goal is to start early and be regular in your
investments. What if you are already in your later years?
Just start where you are and build the discipline to put some

money into investments each month. Earlier is better, but being late to the party is no reason to skip it altogether.

Don't expect miraculous gains. Simply invest what you can each month and leave it alone to mature and grow. While you may need to tend to your investment selection from time to time, don't freak out when the markets adjust and investments lose value. If you are in it for the long haul, just keep looking forward and don't lose your momentum.

Embrace your inner tortoise. Slow and steady.

67

AUTOMATE YOUR INVESTMENTS

I f you have decided to pay yourself first (#64), the next logical step is to make it happen automatically. If you don't have to think about it each month, you are more likely not to fall off the discipline wagon.

Do you have a retirement plan through your employer? If it is a 401(k)-type plan and you are funding it, then you are already following this advice! If you aren't funding it yet, then that is the easiest place to set up automatic investing.

Don't have a plan available, or you are already funding your plan to the maximum? Good for you if the second scenario applies! If you don't yet have a plan, you can establish your own retirement account (an IRA or Roth IRA, subject to some limitations) and set it up to draft a set amount each month directly from your checking or savings account. The money then goes straight into an investment plan that you establish with the company sponsoring the account.

How much should you invest each month? It all depends on the budget or spending plan that you've devised. In general, I suggest starting small and doing a slow build. For example, let's say you studied your spending and you think you can curb expenses to generate $100 per month toward investments. Start with $50 and let that go for a few months. If you don't miss it and feel you can do more, bump it up to $75 or $100.

The key to success with this plan is to reevaluate at regular intervals. If you are comfortably affording the current level of investment, raise it. If you do this consistently, you will be saving significant amounts of money each month. And don't underestimate those small amounts—*all* amounts grow over time!

68

INVEST IT
AND
FORGET IT

Once you are an investor, you may feel that your financial situation is more complicated and requires much more of your time and energy. This is flawed thinking. Do not make the mistake of investing your money and constantly tinkering with it. Invest it and forget it. With some caveats, of course.

Do the work at the front end to find the appropriate asset allocation for you (#69). Then, if you are doing it yourself versus working with a professional, choose index funds to fill out your allocation (#72). Then once every year or so, recalculate your allocation categories and rebalance your portfolio. For example, if it was a good year for stocks and your 50% stock, 50% bond/fixed portfolio is now 60/40, sell off 10% of your stock assets and reinvest the proceeds into your bond/fixed assets.

Depending on where you have your investments, there might even be the option for automatic rebalancing. If you have a very small portfolio, consider using one investment (typically this would be a mutual fund) that holds both stocks and bonds, and it will rebalance itself.

I am not saying you should never look at your portfolio choices. It is prudent to do so. The problem with paying *close* attention to your investments is that you are likely to notice that one is not performing well, and suddenly there's an urge to replace it with something that is performing better. This is often a mistake. Not all categories of investments perform well every year, so this might just be an off year. Don't abandon your well-planned allocation in the face of a bad performer. See how it does in follow-up years before you pull the plug.

The best approach novice investors can take is to invest it and forget it—but rebalance once in a while. If you are invested in index funds, there aren't "underperforming managers" to weed out of your portfolio. Stop worrying about it. Go find something else to pay attention to.

You know the old adage that a "watched pot never boils?" If you basically forget about your portfolio, you might just be surprised at how well it does without your constant oversight.

69

USE A SIMPLE
ASSET ALLOCATION

A sset allocation is a fancy way of talking about diversification. And diversification is a fancy way of saying, "Don't put all your eggs in one basket." If you are going to invest, develop a plan for how much risk you are willing to take. This process can be both a science and an art, and many folks prefer to work with a professional to establish and maintain an appropriate allocation.

If you are doing it yourself, however, try to keep it simple. Many investment sites offer quizzes to help you determine your risk tolerance. This produces your "risk profile." Different places may use different terminology, but you may find you are a "conservative" investor or perhaps a "moderately aggressive" investor. Determining your risk tolerance is important, because it directly informs what investments you will choose for your portfolio. Investments with greater risk generally offer greater return. Those with lower risk will correspondingly offer lower returns.

Risk tolerance depends on a variety of factors. Your age and your proximity to the goal at hand are starting places.

The younger and/or farther away in time you are from when you need the money, the riskier you can make your allocation. Perhaps you've had past experience in investments (good or bad) that will color your view of how much risk you are willing to take. This is where the art comes in: choosing the perfect allocation.

Don't let worry stall you. Complete an online quiz. If you are uncertain between two allocations, let the time horizon be the guide. Longer time horizon? Choose the more aggressive of the two. Shorter time horizon? Choose the less aggressive of the two. Unless you are willing to get professional help on this, the trouble you may run into is analysis paralysis. Pick one and invest. And then leave it alone.

You should review your allocation choice intermittently to make sure it is still appropriate for your needs. A change in your time frame, a big market correction, or other goal changes might be catalysts to reevaluate your risk tolerance. Did you freak out when the market plummeted? Perhaps you need to dial down your risk. The important thing is to wait for recovery before you adjust it. Selling out when the market is down is the surest way to be unsuccessful with your investments.

70

CONSOLIDATE YOUR INVESTMENTS

Today, it is common for people to change jobs. Back in our parents' or grandparents' day, a worker often started with a company and stayed with that same company for the rest of his or her career. Not so any more.

In addition to the general life disruption that occurs when you change jobs, a side effect often develops—old retirement plan accounts. One of my clients had changed jobs several times over the span of a decade, and he had five (seriously, five!) old 401(k) plans scattered about the investment universe.

While there is nothing inherently wrong with having multiple accounts, it is definitely not simple. Spend an afternoon gathering up all your account statements. Sort them into piles by the type of investment. Most forms of employer retirement plans (401(k), SEP, SIMPLE IRA after 2 years, 403(b), etc.) can all be combined into one account.

If you are currently employed at a business with a retirement plan, you have a choice to make. Ask your plan provider if you can roll other old retirement plans and traditional IRAs into your current plan. Your second option is to combine all those old accounts into one new account either at a broker- age firm or mutual fund company. This would be a "Rollover IRA" account. Generally, all accounts that have only pre-tax money in them can be combined this way.

Choosing between those two options? The most stream- lined choice is to roll them all into your current employer plan. But be vigilant and only do this if the investment selection you have in that plan is robust. If you aren't sure or don't want to take the trouble to find out, either combine them all in a Rollover IRA yourself, or work with a professional to make this happen.

What if you have various accounts that are NOT retire- ment accounts? Those, too, can be consolidated. Your best bet will be to transfer them all into one brokerage account. I say "transfer" because you don't want to sell the investments before moving them, as that is likely to generate a taxable event. You just want to move the investments "in-kind" to one central account to streamline your financial life.

When it's all done, say goodbye to all the paper you won't be getting anymore, thanks to eliminating accounts!

71

INVEST IN FUNDS
INSTEAD OF
INDIVIDUAL STOCKS

B uilding your investment portfolio with individual securities or funds is an individual decision. But if your aim is to simplify your financial life, look toward funds.

What is a fund? There are two main types of investment funds—mutual funds and exchange-traded funds (ETFs). Both are similar in their construction: They feature a basket of securities, typically stocks or bonds. So, instead of trying to diversify your portfolio by buying 15 to 20 different stocks, you buy a stock fund instead. Funds have anywhere from a few dozen to a few hundred stocks in them, so they offer more diversification for your investment dollars immediately. You are in essence pooling your money with other investors to buy a broader array of investments in your portfolio, and that can reduce your risk.

Whether you use ETFs or mutual funds is also a personal choice. The main difference between them is how they are traded, which shouldn't matter to a long-term, hands-off investor. If you are using index funds (#72), there are both mutual funds and ETFs that will fit the bill. Both should be extremely inexpensive.

If you want to study up on stocks and buy individual companies, by all means go for it. But if you want to get strong diversification with almost zero hassle, go with a fund.

72

DOING IT YOURSELF?
STICK TO INDEX FUNDS

There is a tremendous amount of discourse in the personal finance arena in recent years suggesting that passive, or index, investing is superior to active management. I disagree with that sentiment. However, there is an exception: less sophisticated investors who are investing on their own.

One investment company has done a masterful job over the past several decades advertising with the message that the cheaper the mutual fund, the more you make. I also disagree with that sales pitch, but I'll stifle my argument. Not coincidentally, that company is known to have among the least expensive funds around, and most of their funds are index funds.

An index fund is built to buy all the stocks or bonds that are currently in a particular market index. Consequently, there is no management team behind the scenes doing research into companies and making active decisions whether or not to hold a particular stock or bond in the portfolio. Since no real decision-making is going on, these funds are cheaper than actively managed funds.

It may have been that fund company who started the notion that "80 percent of actively managed mutual funds underperform their corresponding index fund." I actually agree with that assessment! However, as a proponent of using actively managed funds to reduce risk in portfolios, be aware that the trick is to find the 20 percent of active funds that are routinely beating their indexes!

Unless you are a professional investment manager or an amateur who has the desire and wherewithal to spend the hours necessary in research, the odds are not in your favor to consistently find the investments in that 20 percent category.

The lesson? As a do-it-yourself investor, stick to index funds.

73

SIGN UP FOR
ONLINE INVESTMENT
STATEMENTS

Once you eliminate a bunch of paper by getting your bills online instead of on paper (#23), do yourself a favor and do the same for your investment account statements. Each time you get a statement in the mail from any of your accounts, see if the account is eligible for online access.

This not only eliminates unnecessary paper; it also facilitates your efforts to "invest it and forget it" (#68). Not having paper statements to look at each month or quarter might help you avoid over-analyzing your investments.

Additionally, see whether any of your investment providers offer account aggregation. Sometimes you can "attach" your various accounts to one online access and see all your accounts in one place. You are not actually moving the accounts or consolidating them (although that's something to consider (#70)), you are just giving the main site access to see your other account holdings and values. Doing this makes it super simple to review your accounts once or twice a year.

If you don't have access to account aggregation with one of your existing accounts, look for a financial management app, which would allow you to attach your investment accounts (and pretty much all financial accounts, if you'd like) to one place for easy review and reporting.

Do yourself a favor and markedly reduce your exposure to financial news, especially if it worries you or makes you anxious. It does your health no good to have the added anxiety of worrying about what is going on in the financial world at any given moment. Set your goals, start investing toward those goals, and think long and hard before you derail your plan over some short-term news.

Remember that over long periods of time, investments in the markets (both stock and bond markets) go up. Also remember that over long periods of time, stocks outperform every other financial asset class. Recognize that markets move up and down. Don't put money you know you'll need in a short period of time in the markets! Put your long-term money there, and then just ignore it (#68).

Have a cup of tea instead of watching that news.

You're welcome.

74

IT'S 98 PERCENT
HOT AIR

O f course, this is not a scientifically computed statistic. But it *is* my observation about financial media. There are pundits everywhere you turn, trying to convince you they're financial experts. The influence of media is one of my hot buttons, largely because media pundits usually ramp up the anxiety of the average consumer.

The best way to deal with financial news is simply to ignore it.

If you must keep abreast of what is going on with the economy, find reputable sources to follow. Preferably, these would be non-partisan sources, not on the main networks. The big networks are now all about "info-tainment" rather than being sources for important news.

Also, consider finding investment gurus to follow who have long track records, such as Warren Buffett. If you want to learn a lot about investing and how to massively succeed in your financial life, look no further than Buffett. He is the absolute best role model for living simply, living well within your means, and being a careful but consistent investor.

Simplify Money for Your Kids

75

REIN IN THE
"I WANT" EARLY

Kids are hard-wired to want stuff. It is a pretty rare child who can endure an entire day of shopping without a single, "Ooh, I want that!" As a matter of fact, that child might not exist! The key is to recognize this fact and work with it. It is going to happen, so prepare your strategies in advance.

The goal here is to teach restraint, to help your child understand we don't always get what we want, when we want it. The lesson is manifold: We must work to earn money, and it is that hard-earned money that buys us the things we want and need. And that is key, the idea of *wants versus needs*.

Understanding the difference between a need and a want is also a step toward raising money-mindful children. Raising thoughtful, mindful children is simple, but not easy. Start early to instill the concepts of what is a need and what is a want. As soon as children are old enough to start asking for things when you are out shopping, begin to gently direct the conversation. Say something like: "Today we are only shopping for things our family *needs*, not for things we just would *like* to have."

Repeating this message over the years will eventually reap the reward of more mindfulness. But if you want this to make a lasting impression on your child, take it one step further and model this behavior yourself. While shopping with your children, talk to yourself out loud: "Do I really *need* this, or do I just *want* this?" Determine that it isn't really a need and put the item back on the shelf. Children pay attention to the things their parents do, so make sure they see you walking your talk.

Despite the multi-faceted aspect of this issue, the focus should be on reining in the wants. Sometimes it's effective to simply state before entering the store, or perhaps before even getting in the car to go to the store, "We are going to the store to buy X, and that is it." Or another way to say it is, "I know you always find things you like and want to buy, but I need to let you know that I am not buying anything that is not on our list today." And sometimes simply asking my daughter, "Do you *want* that, or do you actually *NEED* that?" is enough to get her back on track and in touch with reality.

Gift-giving season is another excellent time for this conversation. Help your children develop their Christmas or birthday list by asking the question or encourage them to come up with ideas for gifts they need, as well as gifts they want.

Whatever strategy you devise, work on consistency. If you create a structure your child can count on, this approach will go a long way. On the other hand, if you set up the expectation of no whimsical purchases, only to overturn it to stop their whining, you have taken two steps backward. Remember that your word is your bond. With children this is no different. If you say "no," mean "no" *and don't backpedal.* You know that kids will always look for ways to get what they want (they're not greedy or evil, by the way, they're just kids!), so anticipate it and benefit from that insight. Otherwise, you will be surprised by their flank attack and lose the battle that day—setting a bad precedent for your next shopping trip.

An additional benefit of helping your kids learn to distinguish between wants and needs, of course, is becoming more mindful yourself and developing a stronger sense of your *own* wants and needs.

76

TEACH YOUR CHILDREN
HOW MONEY WORKS

Once for our client newsletter, my team and I all asked our kids some questions about money. How does it work? What does it mean? Why do you like it? These were children ranging from two to nine years old. The answers were, as you might expect, a riot.

Talking to your children about money and how it works is a powerful tool in preparing them to handle their economic lives later. It doesn't have to be boring or pedantic. And it also shouldn't be overbearing.

Here are a couple of examples of how to keep it real while making it interesting.

First, take your kids into the bank with you when you go. Ask them if they know what a bank is for. Explaining that this is where people store the money that they have earned goes a long way toward demystifying how all the cash in your wallet suddenly shows up.

Similarly, when you drive up to an ATM machine, ask your children if they know what you are doing. *If you ask rather than just tell, your kids will be more engaged and interested in the real answer.* Explain that this is not a magical money box. This is a machine that helps you take money out of *your* own account. And the money doesn't just appear. It's in your account because you worked hard and earned it.

Regularly remind kids that money is not handed out. Money is earned through work. We cover allowances in (#78), but whether you offer an allowance to your children or not, start early by giving them the opportunity to do a job for you for payment. Remember, very young children don't have to be paid in cash. They're thrilled to earn jellybeans, or perhaps tokens they can save up to buy a coveted toy.

You're teaching them two important concepts: First, money is created through work. Second, money is used in transactions. As children get older, you can introduce the idea that money can be stored, through saving and investing. This allows us to have money when we need it later in our lives.

Don't blow all of this out of proportion. Just pay attention for opportunities to help your kids get a good, early introduction to what money truly is. While it might be fun, nobody wins when we purposefully mislead kids by walking up to the ATM and waving our hands saying "Look, I press some buttons, and money magically appears out of this box!"

77

START MINIMALIST BEHAVIORS EARLY BY DECLUTTERING

One of the biggest challenges of our modern-day society is the bombardment of noise. Noise takes obvious forms like background music or television, but it also encompasses the constant onslaught of advertisements we see everywhere: on television, the internet, billboards, and bus stops. So much information is channeled into our brains on a daily basis, sometimes it's hard to find the presence of mind to focus on what's really important. Leaving the extraneous and superfluous behind and getting back to your centered self is an act of decluttering.

Teach your children this important practice with a hands-on exercise: In our house, we call this purging. We are referring to reducing our belongings, of course! When my daughter was very young, I would routinely cull through her toys and gear and eliminate what was unloved and no longer used. Between being the only grandchild on both sides, and having newbie parents, there was a lot of decluttering that needed to happen.

At least once a year when she was very young, I would find a time when she was occupied, and I would head upstairs to start filling a bag or a box. Clothes were easy, and outgrown items went right out the door. When it came to toys, however, I was more cautious. Occasionally I'd put some toys in a bag and stash them in the closet just in case she missed them. Of course, she never missed them, although on one or two occasions she would reminisce about some toy she "used to have." She wasn't complaining, she was just remembering.

When she was about four years old, I asked her to help. I suggested that to make room for the new toys that would surely come at Christmas, we should find five toys to give away to less-fortunate children. She was surprisingly game for this activity, so we set to work. In the end, we had three boxes full of things she was ready to part ways with—she was a purging machine. I always asked if she was sure she was done with this toy or that toy, and she was always confident in her choices.

And a new minimalist was born! Now that she is older, she is frequently the one who initiates a purge. "Mom, can we purge my closet today?" Music to my ears.

If your child balks at the idea, keep at it. I asked a few times and got resistance before I used the occasion of Christmas to declutter. Be respectful of your child's wishes and start small. If you build in the habit early and stay consistent, your children will learn that decluttering is an empowering act and nothing to dread.

78

SIMPLE
ALLOWANCES

Opinions vary about if and how you should give your children an allowance. Personally, I am in favor of it for a variety of reasons. In our family, as soon as our daughter was old enough to understand the basics of money, we started giving her an allowance. When she was young, paying her allowance could be haphazard and unscheduled. Now that she is old enough, she's quick to remind me when I forget to give the allowance to her.

Some advocate tying the allowance to specific chores in the house. In other words, if you complete all your "work," you get your allowance. Others think allowance should simply be part of being in the family and not tied to specific work. Developing your child's work ethic is extremely important (#80), but my husband and I decided to give our daughter an allowance that is not tied to her chores. We reasoned that the adults in our house get a monthly allowance as part of our budget. It seemed philosophically in line to give our daughter the same courtesy. And, by the way, she still has chores.

If you decide to give your kids an allowance, make the system simple. We tried an elaborate system once, complete with a chore chart and tally marks, but it was too burdensome. Just find what works for you and your family. We settled on a straightforward system: On a per week basis, our daughter gets one dollar for each year she's been around. So, at eleven years old, she gets $11 per week. She receives a month's worth—or in this case $44—the first of each month. (For the sake of convenience, we ignore the fact that some months have more than four weeks.)

Our daughter gets to spend her full allowance however she pleases (just as we do), but money she earns (#79) gets divided. Half she gets to spend, and half goes toward saving and giving. This, after all, is the way the real world works. *You never get to keep all the money you earn!*

We also give her opportunities to earn *extra* money around the house. She has regular chores that we expect her to do without compensation, such as emptying the dishwasher, helping with the laundry, and assisting with pet care. She rarely grouses, but when she does, we remind her that she is part of our family, and it is her duty to her family to help with household tasks. Occasionally, we have larger projects for which we need her help, and we offer to pay her. Since she is now highly attuned to the value of having money, she almost always agrees to the work.

Find the allowance system that is right for your family. Just be sure to be consistent with your messaging about how an allowance is earned.

79

TEACH YOUR KIDS ABOUT SAVING AND INVESTING

We established an early rule: We ask our daughter to save part of all money she earns or receives as gifts for birthdays and holidays. Her allowance is entirely hers to spend, but half of the earned and gifted money gets set aside for giving (#84) and saving.

When we started this process, we had her divide that money in half—half to spend, and the other half in three parts for giving, saving, and investing. However, since making investments can require a minimum amount to contribute, this became overly complicated. So we streamlined it: Half is for spending and the other half is set aside for savings and giving. Some of the savings and giving money goes into the "give jar," and the rest gets deposited into her passbook savings account.

She is old enough now to come with me to the bank to fill out her own deposit slip and use the calculator to compute a total if she has more than one check to deposit. We let her choose the amount to put in the give jar, and that waxes and wanes. Our intention is to get that back to a formal amount.

Once her savings reaches a few hundred dollars (perhaps once a year or so), I discuss investing with her. We withdraw a portion of the savings and put it into her investment account. When she was old enough, I explained to her what stocks are, and that when you own a stock, you are part owner in the company. (While I am in favor of owning mutual funds in lieu of individual stocks (#71), I make an exception here. We are talking about small dollars in the grand scheme of things, and I want her to have a better understanding of what investing really is.)

When it is time to invest, I ask her to think of things she likes, and I might help by prompting with a few kid-friendly company brands. We settle on companies that interest her, and she is now the proud owner of several stocks!

Since I invest money for a living, this was an easy process for me. If you choose to buy individual stocks, it will require a bit of legwork. Check out online brokerages for lower transaction fees, or better yet, join a credit union. Many credit unions now offer inexpensive investment opportunities. If all else fails, find a mutual fund company that allows for a low initial investment to get started. A quick Google search will get you there quickly.

The bottom line here is to get savings and investing to be a regular part of your child's life. If from an early age they understand the importance of setting aside some of their money for later use, they will be ahead of the game when it's time for them to leave the nest and fly on their own.

80

INSTILL A
GOOD WORK ETHIC

Generational pessimists routinely remark, "Kids today are too coddled! Too spoiled! Today's kids don't know the value of hard work!" To some degree, I think there is truth to this. Our parents and grandparents were raised to understand that work was a normal, everyday part of life, and everyone in the family was expected to participate. But our lives are different than our parents' and grandparents' generations. Today, in many households, much of the work around the home is outsourced.

In terms of raising well-rounded, well-equipped kids, I think this is a mistake. Our kids need to learn about work, and they also need basic skills for living. As a result, I am a huge fan of putting children to work. Even at a young age, kids can start to be held responsible for the messes they make and learn to take care of the things they own.

Does this mean I never do anything for my daughter? Gracious, no. I frequently need to prevent myself from falling into the trap of, "It's just faster if I do it myself." I've had to consciously work to retool that knee-jerk reaction and hold my child accountable for things she ought to be doing.

Start by choosing age-appropriate chores for which your kids are responsible. Whether you pay them an allowance for it or not (#78) is irrelevant. Hold them accountable, praise them heavily for work well done, and up the ante as they age. Don't tolerate complaining and drive home the lesson that work comes before play. "Hey, we are all part of this family, and as part of this family, there is work to be done in the house." Some version of this is an oft-repeated lesson in our house, and it's a worthwhile mantra.

Just as I like to explain to kids where money comes from (#76), I like to remind my daughter why work is important. We homeschool, and I typically only go to the office three days per week. Some days, my daughter whines about my having to leave for work, but when I remind her that "Mom goes to work so we have the money to buy the things we need and want," she completely understands it. Sometimes she just needs the reminder. Sometimes *I* just need the reminder, too.

We work to bring in money to be able to pay for the goods and services we need. We work to be contributing members to the household. We work to be good stewards of the land. We work to make a difference in the lives of other people and the world. These are all excellent lessons to teach our children.

81

SELF-EMPLOYED?
PUT YOUR KIDS
TO WORK!

I f you work for yourself, consider hiring your kids to help you. You'll benefit from the extra hands, of course, but your kids will gain basic knowledge about running a business and managing their finances. If they grumble about boring tasks, just remember they'll thank you later— and for the rest of their lives—for instilling financial responsibility in them at an early age.

The legality of this move will depend on the state in which you reside. In our state, children can work in businesses run by their parents. Since we homeschool our daughter, she comes to my office with some frequency. I offered to put her to work so she could earn money, and she was beyond thrilled at the prospect.

On her "first day of work," she got up and dressed in nice clothes, looking all bright and shiny. When my husband asked her to do something for him, she replied, "I can't, Daddy! I can't be late for my first day of work!" Since then, her dress code has gotten more relaxed, but her desire for more important tasks has grown.

She started out emptying the shred bins in the individual offices into the locked shred boxes. She also puts return address labels and postage stamps on mail. We do a monthly newsletter that goes out to more than three hundred people, so on some occasions, that is a pretty big task. Lately, she has proven to my assistant that she can manage the copying machine, so she has been working on document scanning. Some people might think that is horribly boring, but she thinks of it as a promotion!

While she is generally upbeat about her work, her enthusiasm for work is not constant. Sometimes she would prefer to just read when she is at the office. If she has been talking about some item she would like to have, though, I just mention that she will need to earn the money for it. And presto! The enthusiasm returns.

She is learning about work ethic, but perhaps more importantly, she is also learning about the value of her work. A few years ago, she came to her boss (me) and thoughtfully laid out an argument about how she was doing more complicated work now, and she deserved a raise in her hourly wage. Clearly, she had overheard me discussing upcoming performance reviews with my business partner, and she absorbed the concept and applied it to herself. Good for her!

She got the raise, by the way.

Another plus is that because she has earned income, she is eligible to fund a Roth IRA. While I have her save part of her earnings, I fund her Roth myself. Perhaps when she is a bit older, I'll have her use her savings for the Roth, but for now, it is still a valuable lesson for her to build up a savings account for those purchases she would like to make.

82

PLANT THE SEEDS OF ENTREPRENEURSHIP EARLY

E ncouraging entrepreneurial thinking in your children helps them develop problem-solving skills,
creative thinking, self-confidence, and finan-
cial-management insights. And kids love to play at business and start their own businesses. (At least my kid does!)
Challenge your children to produce products and services
that they can develop, market, and sell—even if only to
the family.

Even if you aren't a business owner, as a consumer you
know plenty about how products are sold. Discuss what
makes for a high-quality product. Help them determine
what is appropriate pricing. Teach them how to create products that fill a customer need. But don't lecture! Gauge your
child's interest before you launch into a monologue about
running a business. Quashing dreams is not the goal.

Consider the age of your child, and structure this
development accordingly. If your three-year-old lays out
his rock collection for you to buy one, you certainly should
do that. But as your child matures, don't just play along

with them mindlessly. Use the opportunity to help them build useful skills.

One time, our daughter arranged a table full of things that she wanted us to buy. She called it her store, and it was complete with little signs that listed the price of each item. The prices were all over the board in terms of reasonableness. Nevertheless, we played along.

We offered up little hints here and there about pricing strategy, but it was in context. She wanted to know why I wasn't interested in one particular item. I explained that I thought the price was out of line for the value of the item, and that I would rather spend my three dollars on three smaller items. She took it all in without comment, but adjusted her prices before Daddy came to shop.

The point is, never discourage them, but instead, find ways to offer little bits of advice to help them improve their skills. Building entrepreneurial skills will help with all areas of their life. Things like addition and subtraction and money handling are obvious skills. But things like discernment and confidence are skills that can also be taught in the context of interaction and exchange. What better way to approach life lessons than through the excitement and satisfaction of making some money!

Children have a natural curiosity about most things, including money, so capitalize on that curiosity. If they don't come to entrepreneurism on their own, offer subtle suggestions. If they just created something (perhaps a greeting card or bookmark), casually suggest that it is nice enough that they could probably sell it if they made more. Usually, they'll disappear for a few hours to start production immediately. You can ask them if they would like some help learning how to market their product.

And away they go!

83

THE MAGIC WORDS: YOU'LL NEED TO USE *YOUR* MONEY

So you've whipped your kids into financial shape: They understand needs and wants, they get an allowance or do chores for pay (or both), and they understand how to save money. This is where the magic happens!

One day, while you're out shopping, your child sees a **SHINY THING** that she just *must have*. You ask some questions: "Do you really need that, or you just want that?" "Why do you want that?" That's my first step—trying to get my daughter to think about and articulate exactly why she wants that particular thing and what purpose it would serve her.

If your questioning hasn't brought about sanity, and your child is still adamant about having it, simply sigh and say, "Well okay, but you will have to use *your money*." Then watch the wheels turning as the child digests this nugget. Suddenly, the stakes are higher than anticipated.

My success rate with this is about 75 percent. About a quarter of the time, my daughter endures the pain of spending her own money and buys the thing. But most times, she realizes that it just isn't worth it to her. Magic!

All you are doing is helping your children apply the criteria you have been preaching all along. Is this truly a need, or is it a want? And if it is a want, is it a whimsical want because it happens to be right here, right now, or is this something you have been wanting all along? We are teaching discernment, and that is a life-long gift that will serve them well as they mature.

84

TEACH YOUR KIDS ABOUT THE POWER OF GRATITUDE AND GIVING BACK

P racticing gratitude on a regular basis is one of life's essential values, but it is also the source of great personal growth and development. We have much to be thankful for in this life. Regardless of our present circumstances, chances are good that we are all better off than many, many others in the world. No matter how lousy you think things are at the moment, don't forget to step back and be grateful for all that you have.

Empower your kids by helping them to develop a gratitude practice. Encourage them to start a gratitude journal. Ask them what five things they are grateful for when they wake up in the morning. Teach them the value of meditating on gratitude, taking the time to focus on it as a part of their daily routine.

In developing your kids' gratitude practice, I'm particularly fond of Arianna Huffington's book *Thrive*, where she suggests simply counting your blessings on your fingers. When you tuck them in at night, ask your children to count five things that they are thankful for. And it's also a good idea for you to do this with them. Use your fingers to keep the tally, and of course, don't discourage them if they want to go to ten things.

Use icky moments when your child is acting bratty or entitled to remind him or her of gratitude. My daughter is pretty well-behaved, but occasionally she loses her senses and slides into entitlement talk. "Listen, Sister," I say ("Sister" is my nickname for her, and it works extra well in situations like this.), "You have nice parents, a nice place to live, clothes to wear, and good food to eat. Not everybody does, so maybe you should check yourself and be grateful instead." Say this in your own way and in your own words. The point is to counteract entitlement with gratitude.

Along with gratitude, of course, comes the gift of giving back. And instilling the value of giving back is critical to your kids' healthy emotional (and financial) development. Because we are blessed with enough, it is our responsibility to give back so that others can have what they need. My husband and I try to repeat this lesson often to our daughter. As I mentioned, we have her set aside some of her earnings to put in her "Give Jar." We're working on being more consistent with this practice, but we try to introduce it as regularly as we can.

While we do include our daughter in our decisions of where to donate money, the Give Jar is totally her gig. She decorated a label and put it on a regular mason jar. We then cut a piece of card stock in a circle to replace the metal top that fits under the screw ring. In that circle, we cut a slot that is large enough to accommodate coins and bills that are folded into fourths. She adds money to the jar, and then each year near the holidays, we have her empty it and count it up. This becomes her donation to a charity of her choice.

If we can tie her donation to volunteering time, all the better. She has done several stints of volunteering for a local animal rescue haven. Now that she is older and more capable, we are actively (and jointly) looking for other ways she can give of her time as well as her money.

Even if the donation your child manages to accumulate is no more than a few dollars, follow through. Get your child to package up his or her donation and, when possible, physically take it into the charity's office. The extra effort on your part to see that your child participates in the entire process is well worth it. It will have a lasting impact on their ongoing practice of gratitude and giving back.

Protect
Your Family
and Pay
Your Taxes

85

PAY FOR YOUR
INSURANCE MONTHLY

I nsurance can be a pesky expense because it tends to crop up "unexpectedly" once or twice a year. As a result, an insurance invoice can throw a wrench into your budget. If you want to simplify this, consider paying your insurance monthly. There are two ways to do this.

The easy way is to arrange for your insurance company to auto-draft your premium on a monthly basis. Most companies will be happy to oblige, because they impose a small surcharge for this convenience. Some companies do not charge a fee, so check with your company before proceeding.

If you want to avoid that charge, choose a slightly more challenging way to pay monthly. Set up your own escrow account and fund it with one-twelfth of the annual insurance premium each month. When the premium is due, you have the money to pay it without putting a dent in your regular monthly budget.

Clearly, option two is better for you financially, because you save the monthly surcharge. But it requires discipline. The idea of planning and saving money ahead of time is a recurring theme in successful money management. In order to pay the least possible amount for any purchase, accumulate the money first and pay for the item outright.

Choosing the insurance company's monthly option for the insurance premium is effectively financing the annual cost over a year, and financing always involves an additional cost. If your aim is to streamline your financial life and you lack the discipline or desire to escrow the money yourself, use the insurance company's monthly plan. At least it will prevent the semi-annual blow to your monthly budget when the insurance premium invoice arrives.

86

CONDUCT A REGULAR
REVIEW OF INSURANCE

When it comes to insurance, most of us simply want to "get it done." No one enjoys spending hours researching insurance. But it's important to never treat insurance as a "one and done." While it is adding a task to your list, reviewing your insurance regularly will help simplify your finances over the long run.

Home, vehicle, and health insurance—as well as umbrella liability coverage—should be reviewed annually. When reviewing, look for changes in your circumstances that would merit a change in insurance coverage. Disability, life, and long-term care insurance can be reviewed less frequently. Clearly, if a life event happens in the interim, an immediate review is necessary.

Reviewing your insurance coverage regularly can result in three outcomes. One is that you decide the coverage you have is perfect the way it is. Or you might determine you are over-insured or paying for coverage you no longer need. Imagine your dismay if you avoid the review for a few years and realize you could have saved some serious dough! Lastly, you might determine that some circumstance has changed, and now you are under-insured. Now imagine your *exceptional* dismay if your house burns down, and you find out there's not enough insurance to re-build it.

When conducting your review of home and auto insurance, don't hesitate to comparison shop. If you find a better deal elsewhere, simply approach your existing company and request a price match. It's essential when comparison shopping that you are comparing apples to apples. All coverage should be quoted compared to identical amounts in your existing policy.

Even if you find a better price elsewhere, don't discount personal service. While it may seem economical to go with a company via a toll-free number, remember that should you need to file a claim, it is always helpful and reassuring to have a personal relationship with your agent.

Depending on the price discrepancies in policies, decide which is more important to you—maximum savings or paying a bit extra for personalized service.

87

BE HEALTHY

Health insurance is one of the largest expenses in a family's budget. While there is continued uncertainty about the future of the health insurance industry, we can do one simple thing to minimize our health insurance expenses: Live a healthy lifestyle.

In fact, maintaining excellent health is one of the best ways to simplify your financial life—and your entire life. Managing your diet, exercise, sleep, and stress can have lifetime positive ripple effects. While "eat good food" or "get enough sleep" may not seem like sound *financial* advice, it is. Bad health habits compound over time and can end up costing huge sums of money later in life in the form of higher healthcare expenses.

Sometimes choosing the healthier path is more costly, but often it can be a cost savings. Simple grocery items like fresh fruits and vegetables can be less expensive than pre-packaged, pre-made foods. Shopping at tailgate or farmers' markets might be more costly, but often ripe produce and baked goods are discounted at the end of the day. Healthy eating will take a bit of practice, but it is a habit you can learn.

Maintaining good health also makes sense when it comes to choosing a health insurance plan. If you are generally healthy, have good health habits, and maintain an adequate emergency savings cushion, then consider a plan with a higher deductible. The annual savings in premiums will add up fast.

Taking the necessary steps to good health often feels complicated, tedious, and difficult to do. But getting and staying healthy will ultimately simplify both your financial life and your life in general.

88

WORK WITH A
TAX PREPARER

I have never met anyone who actually enjoys preparing taxes each year. Many people tolerate it, and some are even semi-cheerful about the challenge. But doing your own taxes requires knowledge and the willingness to dig into potentially difficult (and boring) tax forms.

If doing the work of tax preparation is something you enjoy (or even happily tolerate), great! If you are confident in your abilities to prepare your taxes correctly, even better! But if not, don't hesitate to hire a professional. Similarly, not everyone is eager or capable of creating a financial plan and managing their investments, so hiring a CERTIFIED FINANCIAL PLANNER™ professional to help is beneficial (#104).

The more complicated your tax situation, the more I encourage seeking professional guidance. If cost is an issue, consider preparing the tax forms yourself and asking a professional to review them for you for a reduced fee. If your tax situation is very simple but you're not comfortable preparing your taxes yourself, research local opportunities for low-cost tax preparation. When your income is under a certain threshold, you may qualify for free tax preparation through a Volunteer Income Tax Assistance (VITA) program. VITA is an IRS program offered in collaboration with United Way agencies across the United States.

There is no shame in asking for help. There is also no shame in deciding you want to farm out the work of tax preparation, even if you are perfectly capable of completing it yourself. If delegating this task simplifies your life and you can afford it, go for it!

89

SIMPLIFY YOUR
TAX PREPARATION

Whether you prepare your taxes yourself or work with a professional (#88), it's always a chore to gather up the needed documents and information for tax season. Systems and organization can help reduce the burden of tax preparation.

I have admitted I'm not one for elaborate physical filing systems (#34). Some experts suggest creating file folders to store receipts and other papers needed to prepare your taxes each spring. Multiple folders, however, take up more space.

I use the same approach for my all my papers, whether or not they are needed for tax preparation. Initially, I don't think about whether an item is needed for my taxes: It all just goes right into my single "To File" file. When the end of the year rolls around, I pull out all the tax-related paper. That all goes into a single "Taxes" file folder until I am ready to work on my taxes.

When the spirit moves me to work on taxes (and often that spirit comes in the form of the filing deadline), I pull out my tax file and do a quick sort. Papers belonging to each deduction category get clipped together, and all papers related to income get clipped together. I have a routine for completing taxes, so I organize my clipped stacks in the order I'll need them.

In addition to keeping my paper organization simple, I do two more things throughout the year to save time when doing my taxes. First, if I write a check for an expense I know to be a tax deduction (such as a charitable donation or property tax bill), I write "tax" and circle it next to the description in my check register. This makes it faster for me to find the notation if I need it later.

We do a significant amount of charitable giving through-out the year. To keep it organized, I create a spreadsheet. A simple paper chart or list would also work. Using a chart helps me track progress in reaching our goals for giving throughout the year, but more importantly, it makes tax time a breeze when it comes to charitable giving.

The key to simplifying your tax preparation is to create systems that work for you. Too often, the busyness of life leads to sloppy record keeping and paper storage. As a result, when tax season rolls around, we rack our brains to remember deductible expenses, as well as where to locate the proof of those expenses.

Part of the reason my filing system is successful is the fact that it takes up so little space in my desk and requires zero thought as to where to file something. But you can also create individual file folders for your tax paper categories and file items where they ultimately belong the first time. The bottom line is to *know thyself*. If you are a lazy filer (as I am) and let papers pile up before filing them, then use the one-file system.

Finally, right after preparing your taxes, spend a few minutes evaluating which systems worked well and what needs to improve. The best time to establish systems that help simplify your tax preparation is when the process is fresh in your mind.

90

CRAFT YOUR ESTATE PLANNING DOCUMENTS

I t's a common misconception, but estate planning is not just for the wealthy.

Estate planning means getting your affairs in order in the event you become incapacitated or die. Consequently, estate planning is for everyone. While I admit that getting these documents in place is not a simple matter, it is important for your peace of mind. It also dramatically simplifies what your loved ones must accomplish in the event you become incapacitated or die. The good news is, once drafted the first time, subsequent updates will be much less onerous.

What documents do you need? Well, it depends. Everyone needs four core documents: a will, a living will, a healthcare power of attorney, and a durable power of attorney. Sometimes the living will and healthcare power of attorney are drafted as a single document, which is fine.

The living will (also called an advance directive) and powers of attorney give direction regarding what happens to you if you become incapacitated and unable to make decisions for yourself. The living will outlines how you wish to handle end-of-life decisions. Do you want to extend your life artificially if you are in a vegetative state? The living will also specifies how you wish your remains to be handled. Do you wish to donate your organs? Or donate your body to science?

The healthcare power of attorney names the person who has the ability to carry out the wishes you have outlined in your living will. The healthcare power of attorney also grants the power to make healthcare decisions that are *not* covered by your living will. It is wise to name more than one person, in the event your first choice cannot serve in your time of need. Also, give thought to who would be the most level-headed decision-maker. Illness and incapacity are difficult situations, and it is best if you can avoid family conflict by naming a person who can follow your wishes without drama.

Durable powers of attorney are similar, but instead indicate who can act on your behalf with regard to financial issues. This is the person who can file your taxes and withdraw money from retirement accounts for your care. As with the healthcare model, it is wise to name more than one person, in your preferred sequence. Be sure to choose a person with the capacity to handle financial issues and someone who is thorough and persistent. Working through financial issues on another's behalf can be time-consuming and frustrating work.

A will (also referred to as a "Last Will and Testament") is the only one of these estate documents that handles your affairs after you die. Your will outlines how you want your property to be disbursed at your death. This applies to both your real property (e.g., your house and other real estate) and your personal property. You may have some financial assets, such as retirement accounts, that name beneficiaries, which are not governed by your will.

If you have minor children, your will also fulfills another very important role: It states whom you wish to be guardian of your children if you die while they are still minors. This is often a very difficult decision for parents to make (and agree upon!), but the complications if you die with no guidance on guardianship for your kids can be tragic. Do you want court officials deciding who in your family would be the best caretaker for your children? We all have crazy family members who are nice to visit, but not the best choice for raising our kids. Don't roll the dice: Specify your wishes for guardianship.

Estate planning is one of the most dreaded financial tasks there is. But once you do the hard work and have the tough discussions to get these documents in place, you will breathe easier knowing you have simplified things for your family in the event of your demise or incapacity.

Rethink Retirement and College

91

THINK HARD ABOUT
THE RETIREMENT
LIFESTYLE YOU WANT

The long-standing stereotype about retirement would have you work hard for thirty years, receive your gold watch, collect your pension, and retire to Florida to play golf. Or something like that. But getting fixated on a fantasy retirement becomes a big problem when you find that vision is totally out of reach.

I'm not suggesting you shouldn't have big dreams and work toward them. But in our modern environment (no company pensions, workers changing jobs frequently and missing out on years of retirement savings, Social Security not enough to cover expenses), it is important to keep your finger on the pulse of what is realistic when it comes to retirement planning.

As you work toward your retirement years, focus on what feeds you emotionally, intellectually, physically and spiritually. What activities do you see yourself doing? Could you trade golf for a less expensive activity (#48)? If you like being social and involved, will you volunteer or work part-time? Ultimately, you need to answer one question: How much retirement income will you need to fund your desired life?

Think about the way you want to feel when you get up in the morning in retirement. Once you have a clear picture of what you want, you can create a financial plan to get there. Focusing first on the outcome is a far better approach than trying to follow generic formulas for how much is "enough."

If retiring to Florida to play golf is what you want, you might have to work longer or save more to achieve it. As Stephen Covey said, "Begin with the end in mind." Develop a clear vision of your ideal life, and then plan for it. And don't hesitate to adjust your vision along the way if needed.

92

THE
RETIREMENT
TRIFECTA

Want to know the secret to a perfect retirement plan? I call it the Retirement Trifecta: no debt, multiple streams of income, and adequate savings. Piece of cake, right? Not necessarily. But also not out of reach. If you are still working and looking ahead to retirement, keep your focus on ways to improve all three of these areas over the coming years.

Savings: This one is pretty obvious. Taking advantage of all the ways you can to save for retirement through your employer is your best bet. But that might not be enough, so look at the use of Traditional or Roth IRA accounts to further supplement your long-term savings. Don't forget to build a strong emergency fund, too!

Debt: The ideal situation is to retire with zero debt, including no home mortgage. While this may be a lofty goal, strive for it. At a minimum, aim for no debt other than your mortgage.

The rationale for reducing or eliminating debt as you head into retirement is two-fold. Carrying debt is a risk, because you are legally required to satisfy your debts. Having less income in retirement puts you in danger of not having enough to cover all your expenses.

The second reason to reduce or eliminate debt is all about cashflow. When a debt gets paid off, the monthly expense dedicated to paying it off goes away as well. The more you can decrease your required expenses in retirement, the more breathing room you will have in your financial life.

Income: Retirement income streams might include Social Security and government or company pensions. But the more streams of income you can achieve in retirement, the better your position. Can you create a side business of buying properties to rent in order to have passive rental income in retirement? Can you produce work that provides royalty income? Can you develop a side hustle or hobby that can bring in some part-time income in your retirement years? The more varied your income streams, the better!

Although it is not a requirement to achieve the trifecta in order to retire, it does make your retirement more secure. The further away you are from your desired retirement time frame, the more flexibility you have to start getting these three areas in shape. If you are closer to your target retirement date, focus on getting all debts except your mortgage eliminated, and work to create some side income.

93

DON'T RETIRE.
REDUCE YOUR WORK
INSTEAD

I f you'd like to retire someday, you're probably feeling some pressure. Achieving retirement is not an easy task, since so much of the financial preparation falls on us to accomplish! Company pensions are largely extinct, and Social Security isn't enough to keep us afloat in retirement, so our income and savings are critical to reaching a successfully funded retirement.

But what if you haven't saved enough? Change your perspective. Don't think of retirement as a period of NO work. Instead, think of it as a time of LESS work. You still should squirrel away as much as you can toward your retirement savings, but as you are doing that, work on your mindset, too. Get excited at the prospect of designing this next phase of your life.

If you are realizing your retirement is probably not going to mean zero work, make a plan. Start thinking about how you can transition your existing work in a way that allows you to trim back your hours over time. What opportunities exist in your company or in your field that you might pursue? What is your ideal work schedule as you transition? Make a plan and start working on it.

Working longer provides stable income in your semi-retired state, and it also allows your nest egg to continue to grow until it is needed. And before you start to feel sorry for yourself about having a "second class" retirement, realize there are plenty of people who are actually financially capable of a traditional retirement yet choose this version instead!

Keeping your mind and body busy and moving in retirement is critical to overall good health in your later years. Why not achieve that through continued paid employment? Sounds like a win-win to me!

94

CREATE A
SECOND ACT

I f your plan for retirement requires more years of work
than you'd like, consider changing your job landscape.
Instead of slaving away at a career you dislike for
another twenty years, consider starting a second act instead.

What type of work would bring a smile to your face?
Can you make an income doing the work that feeds your
soul? Don't assume you are stuck in your current job forever.
Think about how you can transition from the career you no
longer like to a new one that you find fulfilling.

You might have to go back to school in the evenings or
otherwise gain some training while you maintain your current job. Or you might have to quit your job and start your
new path with a pay cut. Perhaps a beloved hobby could
evolve into a gig that generates a side income until it is solid
enough to be your full-time occupation.

Don't while away your prime earning years in a job you
hate. Spend time dreaming of your perfect work—work that
makes you happy and fulfills you—and then make a plan.
To begin, engage in the work you THINK you might love in

a low-risk way, such as through volunteering or a part-time side job. Once you are certain of your path, march forward with deliberate, thoughtful steps.

Making a change like this might lengthen the time horizon to your target retirement date. But maybe that won't matter! Perhaps your renewed enthusiasm for work will make up for the deadline extension. Or maybe your second act IS your retirement! Not everyone views retirement and leisure synonymously. Your new work may be rewarding well into your golden years.

Part of simplifying your financial life is to always keep your options open. Thinking about other options for the second act of your career ensures you are in control of the quality of your life. It keeps you in the driver's seat.

95

RETIREMENT
IS A STATE OF MIND

We tend to lock in on stereotypical images of retirement: getting the gold watch, playing golf, or sitting on the porch in a rocking chair drinking a mimosa (or maybe that last one is just mine?). In reality, retirement is a state of mind and should be viewed that way.

Plenty of people hit retirement age and never stop working, even though they could manage it financially. Other people "retire" long before retirement age by cutting back their workload simply because they can.

Try to separate the mental aspect of retirement from the financial aspect. We can and should think about money through the lens of *financial independence*. Strive for a time when you've accumulated enough assets and sources of income to cover all of your expenses without the need for paid employment.

Talk about freedom! If we separate the two concepts, we are also separating the objective from the subjective. We can objectively evaluate whether our hard work has generated enough assets to arrive at the point of financial independence. Whether or not we continue to pursue paid employment becomes irrelevant to the situation.

On the other hand, if we are not close to financial independence, we can still have a retirement mindset. We can "retire" from a career track we've followed most of our adult lives and switch gears. We can start a new business or develop a side-hustle. We can cut down to part-time work because we have enough resources to cover the difference. The possibilities are many.

Being stuck in the rut of requiring your nest egg to hit a certain target before you are "free" to retire is depressing and short-sighted. Instead, change your mindset. Choose to shift to a retirement mindset and work out the financial plan that will allow you to finance the life you not only need but *want*.

96

TEST-DRIVE
RETIREMENT

How do you know you are mentally and financially able to retire? There are on-line formulas and computations that will project what your nest egg will be, and if it will be sufficient to cover your needs. More challenging, however, is to ensure you are positive you can live on the retirement income target you have set for yourself.

To avoid making a catastrophic mistake by quitting your paid employment before you are ready for the leap, take retirement for a test-drive. Thoroughly develop your retirement budget and practice living on that amount of income. Remember to make some adjustments for expenses that you currently have that will not be a part of your retirement budget.

For example, let's say you are five years from retirement. If all goes well, your mortgage will be paid off by then, and you have identified a few thousand dollars of current annual expenses that are irrelevant in retirement. Compute your remaining living expenses and count that as your retirement budget.

From your current income, track separately the income that goes toward the expiring expenses, and focus your attention only on the income that goes toward your "retirement" expenses. See if you can stick to that budget for six to twelve months.

Look critically at areas in which you tend to be less careful. Groceries, dining out, entertainment, and travel are categories to watch carefully, as well as any categories you know to be your weak spots.

Once you prove to yourself that you can, in fact, live on the budget you have envisioned for your retirement, you will be more confident stepping into your next chapter when the time comes to end your paid employment.

97

INSTEAD OF SAVING FOR COLLEGE, SAVE FOR RETIREMENT

A s soon as people have children, they feel pressure to start saving for their kids' education. But this societal pressure often leads to poor choices about HOW to save money for college. The best approach is to take a long-term, strategic approach to accumulating college funds, one that dovetails into *your* long-term, strategic plan for retirement.

I always tell parents that they should completely forgo saving for college until they are maximizing their contributions to all available retirement savings vehicles. The reaction is typically shock and horror on the part of the parents. How could we do that?! But stick with me.

When planning for college, it pays to think ahead. Retirement assets do not count as assets available for paying for school, even though some retirement accounts allow access to a portion of your funds for education without penalty. As a result, it really does make the most sense to maximize saving for retirement first. If you still have money you can sock away for college financing, consider using a Section 529 plan to save for college.

Here are the facts: If you haven't saved enough for higher education, you can take out student loans to pay for college. You cannot, however, take out loans to fund your retirement.

98

CONVINCE YOUR KIDS TO CHOOSE A LESS EXPENSIVE COLLEGE

igher education has changed a great deal since I planned to go to college (ahem) a few decades ago. Back then, and for many years afterward, the conventional wisdom was to attend the best school you could get into, regardless of the cost. General consensus was that a top-reputation school would get you farther in your chosen career.

Over the past decade or so, the stories of people experiencing the awful aftermath of this advice are legion. The Great Recession of 2007-2009 was a game changer. People have been completing expensive educations with an enormous student debt load, and their job prospects are not as lucrative as they once were.

Being saddled with tens or even hundreds of thousands of dollars of debt is no way to start your adult life. No wonder so many young adults are left with no option but to move back home.

One answer to this dilemma is to rethink the college planning process. I'm convinced that for most fields these days, where you go to college matters far less than it once did, at least for an undergraduate degree. People who want to pursue specific professions generally need to attend graduate school. My advice is to save your dollars on undergraduate school so you can better afford the graduate school you desire.

For even more savings on college tuition, consider using your local community college system. Where I live, we have a fabulous community college, and maybe you do, too. If your graduating student can cope with the artificial stigma of not leaving home directly for a four-year institution, community college is a great option.

Consider how much money could be saved if you spent your first two college years getting your general education classes out of the way at community college. Most four-year colleges accept transfer credit from community college systems. However, it pays to be sure by confirming this before venturing down this path.

This is also a great strategy for the students who aren't yet sure about what career path they would like to pursue. Spending a little time getting the basics out of the way inexpensively while learning to be a responsible adult might be just the thing your child needs.

In addition, for students who are unsure about following a vocational route versus the traditional college route, spending a few semesters accumulating the general education classes a four-year college requires, but at a fraction of the price, might be a great experience.

Reframe your thinking about what a college degree means, and eliminate the fallacy that a school with a pedigree will provide a better education than one with a lower price tag. There is ample evidence out there to the contrary. Help your children choose a lower-cost education. The result is likely to be a more secure, less debt-ridden start to their adult lives.

99

FINISH COLLEGE
IN FOUR YEARS

I realize this concept can be controversial. I've definitely heard stories about the real challenges for students trying to get all the classes they need, in the right order, to graduate on time. Assuming those stories are accurate, you can approach this goal in three ways:

First, encourage your students to take a very careful, methodical approach to planning their schedules, so they can get the required courses and graduate on time.

Second, your students can strategically use community college courses in the summer months to get the general education classes completed. This will free up time in their regular school schedule to graduate on time.

Lastly, your students can devote the college years to intensive study and take an above-average number of credit hours each semester to finish their degree. This scenario may cancel out their ability to work while in school or at least limit possible working hours.

I used a combination of all three of those strategies

when working on my undergraduate degree, so mixing and matching can certainly work.

Understand that the assumption here is that your children are going to choose a college major and then stick with that choice. That is a big assumption! Spend time giving some loving attention and parental guidance to help your children wisely choose a major they can follow their entire undergraduate life.

Anything that shortens the duration of attendance at an expensive college will pay dividends in the future in the form of hitting the workforce sooner and incurring less student loan debt.

Bigger
Moves

100

THINK ABOUT
YOUR LEGACY

As you work through getting your estate documents in order (#90), don't overlook your legacy. How do you want to be remembered? Do you want to be remembered for the valuable contributions you made to the world through your work? Do you want to be remembered for your generosity through your charitable work? Perhaps your desired legacy is simply that you were a good human being and you also raised your children to be good human beings.

Whatever legacy you desire to leave, consider how this impacts your financial decisions between now and the end of your life. For example, maybe you wish to be known for your charitable works, and yet you seem to run out of money each month before making those donations. Make time with your family to review your budget and current spending patterns to check for alignment with the legacy you wish to create.

Legacy is not just about money, however. You may want your legacy to be mirrored through your creative energies. If you want the book you write or the art you create to provide value and beauty to others after you are gone, are you making time for that creative work now?

Importantly, remember your legacy also lives on through your children and the impact you have on others in the next generations. What sorts of lessons and values do you wish to pass on to improve the lives of others going forward into the future?

Figure out how to carve out the space and time (which often requires some monetary sacrifice) in your life to lay the groundwork for making your desired legacy a reality. Don't be the person who gets to the end of life and feels regret over opportunities lost or missed. Include legacy thinking in your financial discussions now, so you can make room in your budget and your schedule to achieve the lasting legacy you envision.

101

RIGHT-SIZE YOUR HOME

D epending on where you are in your life, it can be beneficial to examine the appropriateness of your housing. Perhaps you've gone through the exercise of examining the benefits and downsides to renting versus buying a home (#103). Now, take a closer look at how you and your family use your house to determine the effectiveness of your space.

Do you use all the rooms in your house, or do you tend to always congregate in the same spaces? Are your rooms too large, given their purpose, or are you in need of larger spaces? Do you have sufficient storage space in your home? Take a tour of your home and make notes about what works and what doesn't.

Make two lists. List number one is your dream list. Ideally, what would your home include? What would perfect your lifestyle and remain within your affordability range? List number two includes your *must haves*. What are the features of a home that you simply cannot live without? For some, it's a roomy kitchen, while for others, it's a reading nook.

Armed with your lists, take another critical look at your

existing space. Could it be adapted to meet your needs? Since moving can be costly, spend some time evaluating what you already have with fresh eyes. Staying put and modifying your home to better meet your needs is often the less expensive route.

If you cannot make your existing space work, or if your current home is too large for your needs, do a little research to determine the cost of changing your housing situation. You might even consider changing locations (#102).

Right-sizing your home can provide numerous advantages. Selling your larger home and buying a less expensive smaller home might provide you with the opportunity to pay down (or entirely pay off) your mortgage. A smaller or different home might require less annual maintenance than your current home. Lastly, a smaller home might be accompanied by smaller monthly expenses, such as your electric or water bills.

We like thinking about having *more*. Having *more* is easy. Having *more* is what most people desire in many areas of their lives. Having more than enough house is possible, and in many cases probable, since we are conditioned to "buy the most house we can afford."

Yes, having more is easy. Know what is harder? Coming up with the parameters for *enough*.

102

MOVE TO A LOWER-COST-OF-LIVING TOWN

Relocation as a way to gain traction with your financial life isn't the right idea for everyone. But if you want to super-charge your financial life through cutting expenses, evaluate whether moving might be a good option. Considering a move may make sense if you live in a very high-cost-of-living area, and your expenses are eating you alive. Even though uprooting yourself and your family might be a costly upheaval in the short run, the decision may make excellent economic sense in the long run.

Reducing the cost of your housing is likely the biggest win from making such a change, but there are other advantages. When you are no longer living in or near a bustling city, you can save on commuting costs, for example. And the "Joneses" in your new community will likely be scaled down, too, so the need to compare and compete disappears or at least is reduced.

Even though your work may make such a move impossible, that doesn't mean you can't explore the idea. If you become convinced that the advantages of a move outweigh staying put, make a pitch to your supervisor. Perhaps remote work could be accomplished for your position, or maybe another position with your company is an option. It never hurts to ask. You might conclude that a new career, along with a new location, is just what the doctor ordered.

A life change of this nature could not only improve your financial life, but also simplify your life overall. A fresh start with brand new opportunities can be very appealing! A slower-paced community and lifestyle might be exactly what you are looking for.

103

RENT VERSUS OWN

Twenty plus years ago, when I started my career in financial planning, choosing to rent a home versus purchasing one was truly heresy. Despite such strong opinions about home ownership in our society, I always felt (and still do) that a decision to rent instead of buy is not black and white. Sometimes it truly depends on the situation.

Many years ago, I consulted with an older widow who had sold the family home and was living in an apartment. She made the move thinking it was the best move for her, given her circumstances. I agreed. However, she continued to doubt her decision, and this doubt was fueled by criticism from her family members. So we ran some numbers.

Your first instinct is to only compare the costs of the actual rent and mortgage payment and conclude that with rent, you are washing your money down the drain. You aren't building equity! (Equity is the amount of the home's value that you actually own, after adjusting for the debt you might still owe to the bank on your mortgage.)

That is a bad idea. A better plan is to create a side-by-side comparison that includes all the costs in both scenarios.

Sometimes rent only includes certain utilities, for example, whereas you bear the full cost of them as an owner.

In addition to the actual costs for the home (the rent or mortgage) and the cost of utilities, be sure to consider other costs of home ownership, such as upkeep of the house and yard. It is also wise to consider the age of the home when thinking about ownership, since an older home could generate more expense as the years roll by.

Once you look at all the numbers, you might find that the cost of renting is lower, or very similar, to owning. The fact remains, however, that with renting, you are not building equity. How important is that? Here are two things to consider.

First, we live in an age during which people have experienced declining home prices. For many decades, that situation did not exist, and thus the idea developed that "home prices always rise over time." In truth, this is not always the case. Where you live has a great deal to do with whether the value of your home will go up.

Second, it is short-sighted, in my opinion, to exclude qualitative aspects of the comparison in favor of only quantitative factors. Consider the hassle factor. Owning a home can be a considerable amount of work. Renting, on the other hand, offers far better flexibility. While there are pros and cons to both choices, it's important to consider all factors, even if they don't equate to dollars in your comparison chart.

If you feel certain you will live in the house for a long period, ownership might be better. On the other hand, if you are building your career and the possibility exists that you will move to another city to pursue a better job, then ownership might become more hassle than it is worth. Stop worrying about what other people think of renting and consider all factors before making a choice.

104

WORK WITH A
FINANCIAL PLANNER

I believe in the value of working with a CERTIFIED FINANCIAL PLANNER™ professional. Clearly, I am biased on this point, but bear with me. On many occasions, I have pointed out that financial planning (and investment management, for that matter) is not rocket science. It is not calculus. But good, thorough financial planning does involve many moving parts. Having an unbiased professional look over your work to find holes, point out mistakes, and offer new strategies can be a huge benefit for simplifying your financial life.

Let me offer a parallel example. You know that you should eat well, exercise, and generally take care of yourself. And if you do all those things diligently, you are far less likely to need medical intervention. Despite knowing these things and doing these things, we still regularly seek the oversight of our doctor, right? We check in, make sure our bloodwork and blood pressure are good, and that we aren't forgetting anything important for our health. We can also check out new ideas for health improvement.

Think of your financial planner as a doctor for your money. A good financial planner spends a fair amount of time asking questions and understanding your values and goals, as well as gathering lots of data. With data in hand and an understanding of what you are trying to accomplish, a financial planner can give you straightforward strategies to help you reach your goals. And when you work with a planner going forward, you have someone to help keep you accountable and on track.

I call that a win. Sometimes just having someone check your work and tell you that you are completely on the right track has significant merit. And you never know: If your financial planner is good, you might get a valuable new idea or two.

Conclusion

LIFE GETS IN THE WAY

You will never be done simplifying your financial life. *What??* Sounds like bad news, right? Just the sort of thing you want to hear at the end of a book full of tips to do just that: Simplify your financial life. But as it turns out, minimalism or striving for a simpler life is really a personal goal. The same goes for simplifying your financial life. No two people will have the same endgame in mind, and no two people will have the same pathway for getting there. You will never be done simplifying your financial life. And that is totally fine!

Both in my financial life and in my life in general, I have been on this simplification road for more than 20 years now! Some might consider that timeframe and conclude that I am a procrastinator, or even a slow learner. But the truth is far more interesting and informative.

The truth is that things are always changing in your financial situation, just like they did in mine. *Life gets in the way.* You might get married or divorced, have children, or finally launch your children from the nest. Maybe you start a business, buy a house, or move across the country. Not only do these life changes bring shifts to your lifestyle, they also frequently bring changes to your finances.

It takes diligence and focus to continuously simplify your

finances. As new life challenges come up, you have to adapt and find new habits or tools to get you to your goals. The truth is that even without major changes, having a simple life and achieving your financial goals require ongoing maintenance.

But there is good news! The process gets easier as you go. While the challenges you experience may vary in intensity, getting your mindset focused and your financial life organized will help you meet subsequent changes with greater ease.

While you may never be completely finished with simplifying your financial life, by systematically addressing the areas outlined in this book, you will be taking positive forward steps toward more streamlined finances. Commit today to adjusting your mindset about money, and begin taking steps to organize and build systems to manage your money better.

. . . .

You can do this. It is simpler than you think.

ACKNOWLEDGMENTS

A heartfelt thank-you to Elizabeth Sims, who listened to my crazy idea about finally writing this book and provided much guidance and editing along the way.

Thanks to Jim Slatton and Jason Marlin, for being my tech gurus. Your help in building the SimpleMoney and author websites has been invaluable for getting the word out about this book.

Thank you to Scott Boatwright and Katherine Langley for putting your formidable proofreading skills to work to make this book the best it can be.

Many thanks from the bottom of my heart to my pre-readers: Ellen Scott Grable, Leia Smith, Angie White, and Renee Robb-Cohen. As part of my SimpleMoney family, your input on the flow and content of the book was enlightening, and your support has meant the world to me.

And last, but not at all least, thank you and love to Greg and Rowan for putting up with my writing obsession for the past two years.

Appendix

SIMPLIFY YOUR
FINANCIAL LIFE
CHECKLIST

Thank you for reading *Simplify Your Financial Life*, and I hope you enjoyed it!

If you would like to have a free printable checklist of all the projects in this book, visit www.simplifyyourfinanciallife.com/checklist

DOCUMENT
LOCATOR

A Document Locator is a list, either on paper or electronically stored, to guide your beloveds to your important papers. If you would like to have a printable or digital version of this tool, visit www.simplifyyourfinanciallife.com/documentlocator

PERSONAL DOCUMENT LOCATOR

Personal Information

Name #1 _____

Social Security Number _____

Date of Birth _____

Name #2 _____

Social Security Number _____

Date of Birth _____

Residence _____

Work Address _____

Safe Deposit Box:

Number _____

Bank _____

Address _____

Where are the Legal Documents?

Birth Certificates _____

Marriage Certificate _____

Baptismal Certificates _____

Medical Records _____

Burial Records _____

Letters of Last Instruction _____

Divorce Papers _____

Social Security Cards _____

Powers of Attorney _____

Will and Trust Agreements _____

Veterans' Papers _____

Living Wills _____

Other _____

Other _____

Where are the Financial Documents?

Mortgage Papers _____

Bank Account Books/Papers _____

Brokerage Firm Papers _____

Stock and Bond Certificates _____

Income Tax Returns _____

Gift Tax Returns _____

Employee Benefit Data _____

Other _____

Other _____

Where are the Insurance Policies?

Life _____

Life _____

Disability _____

Health/Medical _____

Long-term Health Care _____

Homeowner's/Renter's _____

Auto _____

Other _____

Where are the Titles and Deeds?

Automobile _____

House _____

Other Real Estate _____

Cemetary Plot _____

Other _____

Other _____

PERSONAL RESOURCES

Important People

Financial Planner

Name _____

Phone _____

Address _____

Attorney

Name _____

Phone _____

Address _____

Banker

Name _____

Phone _____

Address _____

Employer

Name _____

Phone _____

Address _____

Accountant

Name _____

Phone _____

Address _____

Other

Name _____

Phone _____

Address _____

Other

Name _____

Phone _____

Address _____

Institutions

Bank

Bank Name _____

Bank Address _____

Account Type & Number _____

Account Type & Number _____

Account Type & Number _____

Bank

Bank Name _____

Bank Address _____

Account Type & Number _____

Account Type & Number _____

Account Type & Number _____

Money Market

Financial Institution _____

Address _____

Account Number _____

Savings

Financial Institution _____

Address _____

Account Number _____

Credit Union

Financial Institution _____

Address _____

Account Number _____

Other

Financial Institution _____

Address _____

Other

Financial Institution _____

Address _____

Insurance Policies

Life

Company & Agent _____

Address _____

Account Number _____

Health

Company & Agent _____

Address _____

Account Number _____

Disability

Company & Agent _____

Address _____

Account Number _____

Long-Term Care

Company & Agent _____

Address _____

Account Number _____

Home Owners

Company & Agent _____

Address _____

Account Number _____

Auto

Company & Agent _____

Address _____

Account Number _____

Other

Company & Agent _____

Address _____

Account Number _____

Other

Company & Agent _____

Address _____

Account Number _____

Digital and Social Media Accounts

Primary Email

Address _____

Password _____

Other Email

Address _____

Password _____

Facebook

Username/Email _____

Password _____

LinkedIn

Username/Email _____

Password _____

Twitter

Username/Email _____

Password _____

FURTHER READING

A h, books. So many books. This list is but a small sampling of the personal finance, simple living, minimalism, and mindset books I have read over the past 25 years. The following selections are the books that made the biggest impact on my simple living and financial journey.

CLASSIC FAVORITES ABOUT SIMPLE LIVING AND MINIMALISM

- St. James, Elaine, *Simplify Your Life* (and all her other books)
- Luhrs, Janet, *The Simple Living Guide*
- Jay, Francine, *The Joy of Less*
- Payne, Kim John, *Simplicity Parenting*

CLASSIC FAVORITES ABOUT PERSONAL FINANCE

- Robin, Vicki, *Your Money or Your Life*
- Chilton, David, *The Wealthy Barber*
- Stanley, Thomas, and Danko, William *The Millionaire Next Door*
- Clason, George, *The Richest Man in Babylon*

MORE RECENT FAVORITES ABOUT SIMPLE LIVING AND MINIMALISM

- Becker, Joshua, *The More of Less*
- Becker, Joshua, *The Minimalist Home*
- Babauta, Leo, *The Power of Less*
- Kondo, Marie, *The Life-Changing Magic of Tidying Up*
- Carver, Courtney, *Soulful Simplicity*

MORE RECENT FAVORITES ABOUT PERSONAL FINANCE

- Mecham, Jesse, *You Need a Budget*
- Hirshman, Susan, *Does This Make My Assets Look Fat?*
- Paine, Crystal, *The Money Saving Mom's Budget*
- Richards, Carl, *The One-Page Financial Plan*

MORE RECENT FAVORITES ABOUT MINDSET AND HABITS

- Niequist, Shauna, *Present over Perfect*
- Sincero, Jen, *You Are a Badass at Making Money*
- Rubin, Gretchen, *The Happiness Project*
- Schwartz, Barry, *The Paradox of Choice: Why More is Less*
- Rhimes, Shonda, *Year of Yes*
- Duhigg, Charles, *The Power of Habit: Why We Do What We Do in Life and Business*
- Richards, Carl, *The Behavior Gap*
- Hardy, Benjamin, *Willpower Doesn't Work*
- Clear, James, *Atomic Habits*

To view this list (and my longer list!) with clickable links, visit www.simplifyyourfinanciallife.com/booklist

ABOUT THE AUTHOR

Dawn G. Starks is a CERTIFIED FINANCIAL PLANNER™ practitioner and financial advisor who likes to keep things simple.

When she established her financial planning firm in 1999, her goal was to simplify the entire financial planning process for her clients. After twenty-plus years, Dawn's mission is still to make financial concepts easier to grasp and less intimidating. Her company now manages over $200 million, working with individuals and couples in all stages of life. By making concepts more accessible, she has successfully empowered her clients to find financial literacy and security.

In addition to her commitment to simplifying financial planning for her clients, Dawn has discovered the personal benefits of minimalism and simple living. In 2018, she expanded her horizons with the launch of her online business, SimpleMoney, where she writes and teaches about personal finance and shares the benefits that simple living and minimalism can bring. When she's not writing or working, Dawn is an avid reader. She particularly loves to read about time management, and of course, simple living. Dawn lives in the mountains of Asheville, North Carolina, with her husband and daughter, and a dog, a cat, and five chickens.